"We're facing the most sign_____
last 500 years. *Digital Minist_. _____ _____ __ _____ ____ ____ _____*
presents current and compelling evidence for the use of digital
technology in ministry, and even better, provides practical
ways of using digital tools to integrate and extend ministerial
and faith formation efforts. Church leaders will find this book
to be a source of inspiration and a valuable resource for some
time to come."

> —Steve Botsford, leader in digital catechesis and
> catechetical transformation

"*Digital Ministry and Leadership in Today's Church* blends the
theoretical as well as the practical in an accessible guide for
ministry leaders. The varied perspectives and curated resources
prove helpful for anyone exploring and advocating for a deeper
use of technology in their ministry setting."

> —Andrea D. Chavez-Kopp, education and
> ministry consultant

"Sister Caroline Cerveny's ministry and legacy as a digital
disciple shines through this work. Her death is a deep loss in
the area of digital ministerial formation, and I am delighted
that this volume honors her memory by continuing the
important work of inviting thoughtful theological and practical
reflection on ministry in our digital culture. The result is a
relevant and usable volume for today's ministerial leaders in
our digital world."

> —Daniella Zsupan-Jerome, PhD, Director of Ministerial
> Formation and Field Education, Saint John's
> University School of Theology and Seminary

Digital Ministry and Leadership in Today's Church

Edited by
John Roberto

LITURGICAL PRESS
Collegeville, Minnesota

www.litpress.org

1	2	3	4	5	6	7	8	9

Library of Congress Cataloging-in-Publication Data

Names: Roberto, John, editor.
Title: Digital ministry and leadership in today's church / edited by John Roberto.
Description: Collegeville, Minnesota : Liturgical Press, [2022] | Includes bibliographical references. | Summary: "Provides essential knowledge, practices, and skills to guide pastors, ministry leaders, and faith formation leaders in Christian churches in creating digitally integrated ministry and faith formation in their churches"— Provided by publisher.
Identifiers: LCCN 2022009102 (print) | LCCN 2022009103 (ebook) | ISBN 9780814668023 (paperback) | ISBN 9780814668030 (epub) | ISBN 9780814668030 (pdf)
Subjects: LCSH: Church work. | Christian leadership. | Technology—Religious aspects—Christianity. | Digital media—Religious aspects—Christianity.
Classification: LCC BV4400 .D54 2022 (print) | LCC BV4400 (ebook) | DDC 259—dc23/eng/20220404
LC record available at https://lccn.loc.gov/2022009102
LC ebook record available at https://lccn.loc.gov/2022009103

Contents

Dedication

*Sister Caroline Cerveny, SSJ, TOSF (1943–2020),
Founder of the Digital Disciples Network*

Sister Caroline Cerveny, SSJ, TOSF, was and is a great gift in my life—not just a colleague, but a fellow pilgrimage leader and more. She was a real friend. This book is dedicated to Caroline because she was and remains a great gift to all of us. In her life and as founder of Digital Disciple Network (DDN), she saw and affirmed the gifts and talents of each of us—often before we saw them ourselves. Moreover, she was really a sister who cared about all the parts of our lives—family, health, challenges, and more. We see that personal care and concern in how she structured the classes in DDN. Each participant had a personal mentor to accompany them and to be very available on the journey through the program.

Sister Caroline was a visionary and way ahead of her time. Back in the early '70s, when personal computers were just becoming available, she already saw their use, along with social media, in education for and from ministers at all levels. Today, when the circumstances of the COVID-19 pandemic have pushed teachers in schools and pastors and other ministers in parishes to learn how to use Zoom and other digital tools, many who knew Sister Caroline remark that she must have a big grin on her face in heaven as she sees her vison of digital media becoming so central to the life and ministry of the church today.

Sister Caroline was also one of the most creative people I have ever met. She always saw the new possibilities and how they could better the programs of DDN. Moreover, she started an Annual Conference in Orlando simultaneous to FETC, the Florida Educational Technology Conference. Her creative edge helped her to appreciate the inspiration and forward-thinking attitudes of leaders in digital ministry and Catholic social media. Caroline also saw the creative efforts of her own staff of DDN, whom she also invited as presenters and discussion leaders. One of the key reasons she chose to have the conference simultaneous to FETC was to expose the DDN participants to the marvels of new and ingenious products in the digital world on display in the great hall.

Caroline was also a woman of living faith. Besides DDN, she led study groups on Franciscan Spirituality and was a co-leader of pilgrimages to the Holy Land, Rome, Ireland, and France. She was also very Ignatian. Besides being a big fan of Pope Francis, she had a very incarnational vision, grounded in the everyday life of faith and ministry, and in paying attention and writing about the new and creative developments in social media for use in ministry and church life.

In reading her biography, friends and others are often amazed at all her accomplishments, including a doctorate and two master's degrees. Often, in proofing articles she wrote, I would remind her to put "Dr." in front of her name as a recognition of her education and competency. But as I close this dedication, it strikes me that she was more comfortable with "Sister Caroline." She wanted to be recognized on the same level as everyone else. She was truly a sister to each of us who knew and loved her. Sister Caroline was and is for us "the great gift beyond price."

Fr. Michael Cooper

Introduction

We have written this book to honor Sister Caroline Cerveny, our colleague in digital ministry and a national leader in bringing digital tools, methods, and means in church ministry and faith formation. We are writing for pastors, ministry leaders, and faith formation leaders in Christian churches who want to initiate, develop, enhance, or grow their use of digital platforms, tools, methods, and media to further their missions and ministries. No matter what your level of confidence, comfort, and competency in digital ministry, you will find ideas, strategies, guidance, and support for your next steps—for you and your church community.

Digital Ministry and Leadership in Today's Church provides essential knowledge, practices, and skills to guide church leaders in creating digitally integrated ministry and faith formation in their churches. Digitally integrated ministry has a dual focus: (1) bringing digital approaches, tools, methods, and media into church ministries (worship, learning, prayer, spiritual formation, and more) and (2) extending the ministry of the local church (spiritual care, formation, prayer, service and social justice, evangelism, and more) into online spaces and communities (Facebook, Twitter, YouTube), where more and more people gather to nurture, explore, and share their faith today. As you will see, the chapters in the book address one or both aspects of digital ministry.

We have designed the chapters of the book around a set of core competencies developed by the Digital Disciples Network and its partner organizations, guided by Sister

Caroline Cerveny, SSJ, TOSF, then president of the network. The competencies describe the knowledge and skills that leaders need for digitally integrated ministry and faith formation. These competencies are fully described in chapter 6.

Chapter 1, "The Digital Transformation of Church," by John Roberto, describes the emerging portrait of how churches are utilizing digital tools, methods, and media in community life and faith formation. The COVID-19 pandemic dramatically accelerated digitally integrated ministry and a more expansive view of church and how people are formed in faith.

Chapter 2, "Digital Tools and Methods for Ministry and Faith Formation," by Tim Welch, provides practical ideas for using digital tools to (1) create a website for a ministry or for faith formation; (2) create and edit short videos for church life and faith formation; (3) create still and motion graphics and utilize them in digital spaces; (4) develop livestreaming for classes, courses, and presentations, and archive videos for use online; and (5) convene a live meeting using interactive digital meeting platforms.

Chapter 3, "Community and Relationship Building in Virtual Spaces," by Deanna Bartalini and Claudia McIvor, provides practical ideas for extending church life and ministries into online spaces with a focus on organizing groups of people online using social media platforms to build relationships, share life and faith experiences, pray for people, celebrate special milestones and occasions, share inspirational insights to encourage people to live with Christlike characteristics in their everyday lives, and more.

Chapter 4, "Faith Formation in the Digital Age," by John Roberto, presents models and approaches for developing hybrid (in both online and physical spaces) and online-only faith formation. The chapter also provides ideas for developing digital playlists of multimedia faith formation content that is interactive and personalized, with a variety of ways to learn and experience the content.

Chapter 5, "Curation of Digital Media for Ministry and Faith Formation," by Marge Babcock, provides a toolkit for developing the skills and processes for curation, including (1) the ability to research and organize digital media and resources from trusted sources, such as blogs, curated Christian websites, denominational websites, and Christian organizations; (2) the ability to evaluate digital media and resources using Christian values and ethical principles; and (3) the ability to connect the best and most relevant resources to programming in gathered, online, and hybrid models of ministry and faith formation.

Chapter 6, "Leadership for Digital Ministry," by William Miller and John Roberto, presents two sets of leadership competencies—knowledge, skills, and attitudes—that pastors, ministry leaders, and faith formation leaders need in today's church communities. The first set describes the emerging twenty-first-century leadership competencies for digitally integrated ministry and faith formation in churches. The second set describes the enduring, foundational competencies that form the basis for effective pastoral leadership in every age and era.

There are many ways to use this book. Chapter 1 provides the introduction and overview—setting the stage for the rest of the book. Chapters 2 through 5 are written as toolkits to guide you in developing digital skills and applying digital approaches to your church. Chapter 6 focuses on you, the leader. You might want to start with chapter 6 to get the "big picture" of leadership for digitally integrated ministry, map your personal learning journey to develop your skills, and then turn to the chapters in the book that will best help you enhance your ability.

Authors and Contributors

Authors

Marge (Margaret) Babcock has many years of experience in faith formation with a special focus on curation and website development within the Roman Catholic Diocese of Syracuse (New York). She also has served in leadership roles, particularly focused on adult spirituality and enrichment.

Deanna G. Bartalini, MEd, MPA, is a Catholic writer, speaker, and educator on the topics of Scripture, prayer, everyday life and faith, and using technology to spread the Gospel. Her Bible study is published by Our Sunday Visitor. Deanna writes at DeannaBartalini.com.

Claudia McIvor is a cofounder of Digital Discipleship Boot Camp. She is the director of faith formation at Saint Mary, Our Lady of Grace Catholic Church in St. Petersburg, Florida.

William (Bill) Miller has worked in educational ministry at the local, diocesan, and national levels for over forty years. He is the author of *Finding Your Spiritual Direction as a Catechist* (New London, CT: Twenty-Third Publications, 2017) and a contributing author to *The Joy of Adolescent Catechesis* (Washington, DC: National Federation for Catholic Youth Ministry, 2017).

John Roberto is the founder of Lifelong Faith Associates (2006), where he is involved in teaching, writing, researching, and consulting in lifelong faith formation. His latest book is *Lifelong Faith: Formation for All Ages and Generations* (New York: Church Publishing, 2022). His resources and articles can be found at www.LifelongFaith.com.

Tim Welch served as the associate director for educational media/technology at Catholic Education Ministries, Diocese of St. Cloud, Minnesota. He is the author of *Technology Tools for Your Ministry: No Mousing Around* (New London, CT: Twenty-Third Publications, 2008), a former columnist on integrating technology into catechesis, and the author of blogs for *Telling Our Story in the 21st Century* at fromtheheartmn.org.

Contributors

Ruth Manlandro, PhD, is an instructional designer, academic coach, trainer at Eduscape Design, and coach at Digital Disciple Network. She is a Microsoft innovative educator expert and master trainer and a Google-certified educator and coach.

Andrea Slaven is the director of catechesis in the Diocese of Syracuse. She has a master of education and an MA in instructional technology. Her studies also include a master certificate in pastoral theology.

Cheryl Smith, a former recipient of the NCCL "New Wineskins Award," is recently retired from many years as a faith formation associate and is currently employed part-time by the Diocese of Syracuse Office of Catechesis as a "media writer." She is also an independent consultant for parishes needing technology assistance.

CHAPTER ONE

The Digital Transformation of Church

John Roberto

When we look back at the past thousand years, it would be safe to say that the invention of the printing press had the most dramatic impact on civilization. It brought about a new age—increasing literacy rates and providing a much wider access to literature in all forms for ordinary people. This new technology made it possible for Martin Luther and the Protestant reformers to bring the Bible into people's homes and daily lives. It made possible the production of catechisms for each Christian tradition, which quickly became centerpieces of religious education for children and adults. The Christian church was an early adopter of the new technology of the printing press and the revolution it began.

In the twenty-first century, the digital revolution, led by the invention of the internet, a wide array of digital tools, technologies, and social media platforms is having the same dramatic impact on society—and the Christian church—as the printing press. The combination of streaming media, video conferencing, websites, online learning platforms, and social media made ministry and faith formation possible during the COVID-19 pandemic.

The invention of digital technologies—and the transformation that is underway—is the "big" story of the early part of the twenty-first century. In their 2012 book, *Networked: The New Social Operating System*, Lee Rainie and Barry Wellman anticipated the huge impact that the "triple revolution"— the rise of social networks, the personalized internet, and always-available mobile connectivity—was going to have on people's lives. They saw that the coming together of these three factors would shift people's social lives away from densely knit families, neighborhoods, and group relationships toward more far-flung and diverse personal networks.

The social networks revolution provided opportunities for people to reach beyond the world of tightly knit groups, affording people more diversity in relationships and social worlds—as well as bridges to reach these new worlds and maneuverability to move among them. The internet revolution gave people communications power and information-gathering capacities that dwarfed those of the past, allowing people to become their own publishers and broadcasters and creating new methods for social networking. The mobile revolution (i.e., the rise of portable, connected devices like cell phones and tablets) fundamentally changed the relationship between information, time, and space. Information became portable, participatory, and personal. People of all ages now create content through social networking sites and other social media, as well as through their various rankings, ratings, commenting, and remixing applications. In an environment where most people are "publishers" and "broadcasters" and where powerful search technologies make it easy to find such content, people can easily locate and connect with others who share their tastes, lifestyles, political beliefs, spiritual practices, health conditions, hobbies, or professional quests.

The widespread practical application of the digital revolution into church life and ministries has been a slow process. There were churches who were innovators and early adopters of the new digital technologies as early as the first decade of the 2000s. They broadcasted their gathered Sunday worship service to an online audience and used social media platforms to connect with their members and with a wider audience—building relationships, sharing faith, praying, exploring social issues, and more. Also, they developed engaging websites which served as the hub of church life and ministries, as well as providing an attractive invitation for people to experience their community. The innovative and early-adopter churches led the way in the utilization of digital tools and media to advance their mission and proclaim the Good News.

The Acceleration of the Digital Transformation

The enforced shift during the worst of the COVID-19 pandemic to virtual working, consuming, and socializing fueled a massive and further shift to virtual activity for anything. One paradox of this shift is that while people were self-isolating and studying or working remotely, many rediscovered social ties—sometimes with more people than before—as they participated in Zoom family reunions, birthday celebrations, and family check-ins, including FaceTime storytelling with family members and friends, virtual dinner parties, and so much more. A grandparent could watch their newest grandchild grow from an infant to toddler using the new digital communication tools. People began to naturally turn to social media platforms to satisfy this most basic of human needs.

The pandemic has accelerated the development of our identities as hybrid people living their lives online and offline. Rather than think of these two as separate, people are now realizing that their lives embrace the in-person (physical) and online (virtual). They are living hybrid lives and now living in hybrid Christian communities, as churches have incorporated digital tools, methods, and media into church life and faith formation. Churches are nurturing relationships, spiritual growth, worship, and learning, and they are engaging in ministry in person and online. Through social media, members are cultivating connections online that are not so different from the relationships that prevailed before the internet and mobile phones.

The COVID-19 pandemic was a game-changer for the use of digital technologies, tools, and media in church life and faith formation. The innovative and early-adopter churches scaled-up their initiatives to address the challenges of the pandemic and the loss of physical gatherings as a setting for ministry. Other churches who had been slow to adopt digital approaches or resisted the digital world struggled to adapt quickly in the face of the pandemic challenges. Many succeeded; many did not.

In the face of the pandemic, churches began to reconcile their concerns about technology with the clear benefits provided by the Internet and digital technologies. "Over the last two decades, researchers studying religion and the internet have highlighted the undeniable benefits that moving different aspects of religious work online can offer religious groups. A growing literature exists that illustrates how moving online can potentially expand religious group influence to a new audience and create unique opportunities for outreach. Embracing technology for religious purposes has shown to be a vital strategy during the pandemic and beyond in the decade to come."[1]

---

1. Heidi Campbell and Troy Shepherd, *What Should Post-Pandemic Religion Look Like? 10 Trends Religious Groups Need to Understand to Survive and Thrive in the Next Decade* (Digital Religion Publications, 2021), 8, https://oaktrust.library.tamu.edu/handle/1969.1/192408.

Signs of the Digital Transformation in Christian Churches

Through the COVID-19 pandemic, many pastors and faith formation leaders have done amazingly creative work in faith formation, reaching and engaging people of all ages with tools and methods and media they never imagined using way back in 2019. Churches began streaming worship into people's homes, developing interactive experiences as part of the worship service, incorporating people's experiences and contributions into Sunday worship, and providing formation activities to extend and deepen the worship experience.

Churches redesigned faith formation programming from at-church classes and programs to at-home formation, family clusters (pods), small groups, and independent learning using digital tools and methods, such as websites, digital playlists, video conferencing, streaming, online classrooms, and social media platforms. This was nothing short of a remarkable transformation in the *how* and *when* and *where* of faith formation.

For churches, the "new normal" means there may never be a full return to business as usual—event dependent, off-line only, fixed time, and fixed location. There have been significant transformations that have emerged through the innovations that churches implemented in response to the COVID-19 pandemic—adaptations that can provide a platform for future growth and development. The digital transformation can help churches thrive in the new post-pandemic world. Here is a brief sampling of the things we are learning.

Churches are using new digitally informed approaches (including tools, methods, and media)—many of which have been available to us for a decade—that the pandemic motivated (forced?) us to use as integral to faith formation. In the past we overrelied on faith formation in *physical* spaces for the majority of our programming (at church, at camps, on mission trips, at retreat centers, in community places, and more), which the pandemic has made difficult, if not impossible. We are now using *online* spaces (websites, social media, online communities, online classrooms, and more) as integral for forming faith. And we are using *hybrid* spaces that combine physical gathering with online content and experiences. Group gatherings (such as monthly programs or classes) at church or family clusters (pods) at home or small group meetings are now combined with online playlists that provide a menu of learning experiences on the theme of the program. In addition to gatherings in physical spaces, hybrid faith formation often includes streaming presentations and demonstrations, online classrooms, and online group meetings in Zoom or other video conferencing platforms.

Churches are offering faith formation in synchronous (real time) and asynchronous (on your own time) formats with online and hybrid approaches—thereby expanding the opportunities for people to engage in faith-forming experiences. We are delivering synchronous faith formation by using physical gatherings, livestreaming, video conferencing, online courses, and online small groups. We are incorporating asynchronous formats using online playlists of faith-forming content, video, and audio programs, online discussion groups (like Facebook Groups), online learning platforms, websites, and more.

Churches are making faith formation mobile—bringing faith formation to where people live using the new digital tools, methods, and media. We are creating playlists of faith-forming content for all ages on a variety of themes for families and people of all ages from children through adults. We have invested time and effort in providing faith-forming experiences online so that people can access high-quality content on a phone, tablet, or laptop.

Churches are using traditional tools in new digital ways. We are redesigning our weekly newsletter (or bulletin) into a content- and connection-rich resource that can be delivered directly to people's inboxes using a service like MailChimp, Constant Contact, or Flocknote. Churches that once relied on a print resource now find they can reach a wider audience with a newsletter delivered digitally, which includes a variety of media content (images, audio, video).

Churches are using social media platforms for connection and sharing. We are connecting and communicating with people of all ages, sharing and discussing faith and spirituality, and engaging people to share what they are learning and how they are practicing their faith through videos, images, stories, and more.

An Expanded Vision of Church

The digital transformation and the COVID-19 pandemic have challenged us to think about the church as virtual, as well as physical. "The pandemic forced religious leaders to wrestle with what is a church when people cannot physically gather together or be place-based. While COVID-19 was difficult for some religious groups, specifically the ones that were Internet-hesitant or Internet-refusers, it proved to be the final push over the edge to join the online community. There are some undeniable benefits that moving online showed to religious groups, which lack of physical resources need not stand in the way from creating a worship gather or community."[2]

We are witnessing an expanding vision of where church and faith formation happens. We've moved from a church-building mindset to a multispace approach where faith

2. Campbell and Shepherd, *What Should Post-Pandemic Religion Look Like?*, 20.

formation happens at home, in online spaces, in small groups, in mentoring relationships, in independent learning, in the world. Church isn't the building; it's the people of God, the community of believers, the Mystical Body of Christ. And it can't be contained by a physical space.

Theologian Dianne Thompson explains that Paul's image of the church as the Body of Christ is virtual and physical. She writes, "Paul drew on ancient depictions of community as a body in order to image the Christian community as the body of Christ. . . . And even though Paul traveled only rarely to be physically present with the church communities through Asia Minor, he remained present with those communities *virtually* through his letters."[3]

Thompson emphasizes the virtual nature of Paul's ministry when she writes,

> Paul himself—even as he spent a year or more being physically present with churches like Corinth before moving on—is nevertheless more often a part of all of the particular local bodies of Christ in a virtual rather than a physical way. This point highlights the inadequacy of thinking about the term *virtual* as meaning *almost*. Paul is decidedly more than almost a part of these communities; he is founder leader, guide, and inspiration to multiple communities simultaneously. . . . Even as he developed many close relationships through face-to-face interactions with members of the churches scattered across the Mediterranean, it is also the case that he was only able to be physically present with them on very occasional visits. That Paul's relationships with the ancient churches are maintained primarily through the back and forth of letters has led pastor and writer Jason

---

3. Deanna Thompson, *The Virtual Body of Christ in a Suffering World* (Nashville: Abingdon, 2016), 11.

Byassee to propose that even in its earliest incarnations the body of Christ has always been a virtual body.[4]

Angela Gorrell in *Always On: Practicing Faith in a New Media Landscape* explains that we now live hybrid lives—online and offline. She writes,

> Recognizing online actions as meaning-filled helps Christian communities to consider our current online and in-person reality in terms of its hybridity, rather than in terms of digital dualism (think of online as virtual and in-person as real). Hybridity describes the coming together of online and offline, media and matter, or more dynamically . . . the interplay between the online and offline dimension. Most Americans live hybrid lives because our online and offline lives have been integrated. Interactions online shape offline experiences, and offline communication and practices shape people's online engagement.[5]

We now live in hybrid Christian communities. "Hybrid Christian communities embody God's love and 'make the message believable' through meaningful conversations and faithful habits that are both in person and mediated, that take place at various times, and that happen in both physical and digital spaces. I do not think it is too daunting for Christian communities to think about their community as being hybrid, given Paul's letters and specifically his use of the metaphor of the 'body of Christ.' Paul's letters are a clear example of hybrid Christian communities since his letters were extensions of his in-person ministry within

4. Thompson, *Virtual Body of Christ*, 40–41.
5. Angela Gorrell, *Always On: Practicing Faith in a New Media Landscape* (Grand Rapids, MI: Baker Academic, 2019), 47.

particular communities and also provided mediated guidance for those communities."[6]

Many Christian communities *are* hybrid Christian communities because they are nurturing relationships, growing spiritually, and engaging in ministry in person and online. Through social media, members are cultivating connections online that are not that different from the relationships that prevailed before the internet and mobile phones.

Looking Ahead

As the internet and its accompanying digital technologies have become increasingly embedded in Americans' everyday lives, the desire and ability to use digital media to help facilitate relationships, enhance our sense of care and value, learn and grow, and enable intimate communication and connection have only increased. This reality has been strengthened by people's experience during the COVID-19 pandemic.

Pastors and church leaders had viewed the church and internet as two separate realities. The COVID-19 pandemic was a catalyst for reconsidering the relationship between the online and offline culture. Developing online ministry (worship, learning, praying, and more) was often viewed as optional to ministry in physical spaces at church. The COVID-19 pandemic demonstrated to churches that doing ministry online as well as offline might be more necessary than previously thought. Technology is now seen as a helpmate of ministry and religious life, extending the reach and personal interaction beyond a single gathering place and religious event. Looking ahead, churches need to see online and offline strategies as complementary or two sides of the same coin.

6. Gorrell, *Always On*, 50–51.

Churches are learning to bridge and blend the social opportunities of digital media that can enhance community building, learning, discipleship, and more in order to help people connect their digital engagement with their offline church experiences. Rather than seeing the internet as a problem for religious communities, it should be seen as a gold mine of resources to enhance church relationships that could revolutionize faith-based communities worldwide.

Many researchers and church consultants have noted that the new relationship forming between religious leaders and technology today represents a hopeful shift. Religious resilience and creativity have been demonstrated throughout the pandemic by the embrace of technology. A willingness to experiment with technology shows an openness to change that could mark a shift toward potentially long-lasting changes and positive approaches to cultural and technological innovations.[7]

It's clear from the experience of 2020 and 2021 that religious communities that are flexible and willing to innovate are in better positions to foster resilience in the long run. Many religious leaders were able to be innovative with the centuries-old traditions and ways of doing church. Churches utilized digital technologies to design innovations that enhanced their current ministries, offerings, and/or operations, as well as creating new initiatives that generated growth or reached new audiences.

Innovation is a continual process. Designing and launching innovations are the important first steps in the process; sustaining and expanding innovations are the critical next steps. To resist the forces that will tempt us to return to the earlier forms of church life and faith formation practiced before the pandemic, we need continual innovation. Our world

---

7. Campbell and Shepherd, *What Should Post-Pandemic Religion Look Like?*, 24.

has changed, is changing, and will continue to change—and the pace is accelerating. Being innovative is the essential skill for church leaders in a post-pandemic world.

Our eyes have been opened to new ways of being church, doing ministry, and engaging in faith formation. We have just begun to tap the potential of the new digital technologies and digitally enhanced approaches to church life and faith formation.

CHAPTER TWO

Digital Tools and Methods for Ministry and Faith Formation

Tim Welch

"Whoever Tells the Stories Defines the Culture"

Psychologist and media pundit Dave Walsh posted a masterful commentary on storytelling in which he offers an amazing insight that can give direction to our ministry of sharing the Good News of God's reign. Even with the rapid change in technology, his 2011 message remains true today: *Whoever tells the stories defines the culture.*

As leaders in Christian communities, we are called to tell the story of Jesus Christ, to live into that story, and to do so in such a way as to inspire others to join us. Our very lives become the story that will be carried on to subsequent generations, beginning the cycle anew.

Indeed, Walsh says that stories teach us who we are and who we want to be. Stories can inspire us to action. The point of this chapter is that ministers need to understand the power of storytelling and the competencies and tools for storytelling. For the purpose of this discussion, it is helpful to think of "story" in the broadest sense. All kinds of digital communication can be considered "storytelling," either because they tell actual narratives or because they communicate content that helps us become the story for future generations to tell. It is helpful, whenever something is put online, to be intentionally mindful of how it is passing on our story, telling a new part of our story, or helping us to live into and shape our story for future generations.

Who is actually telling the stories today? "Since World War II . . . parents, teachers, pastors, elders, authors, and sages have been replaced as the primary storytellers by teams of Hollywood and video game scriptwriters, producers, directors and gamers."[1] The goal of modern mass media is to deliver eyeballs to advertisers. Our goal is to deliver hearts, especially our own, to God and others. We want to be the storytellers.

And there is a sense of urgency as our world moves ever faster, spurred on by the rapid increase in technology and its availability to the masses. Carmine Gallo, professional communications advisor, entitled a 2014 *Forbes* blog post, "If You Don't Tell Your Story, Someone Else Will." Churches are telling their stories, but often, de facto, just to the "choir" that shows up on Sundays (or onto their web pages). Who is telling the stories of these same churches to the masses? It would be interesting to stop someone in the street and ask them what they've heard about Christian churches, especially in the wake of sexual abuse crises. Gallo writes, "A strong, truthful, and authentic story will connect with the public, but it's a long and painful road to correct myths, distortions, and outright fabrications."[2] If churches allow only certain stories written by outsiders to be told widely, that is itself a distortion of who we are.

---

1. David Walsh, "Whoever Tells the Stories Defines the Culture," Spark and Stitch Institute, August 3, 2011, http://tinyurl.com/CL-walsh.
2. Carmine Gallo, "If You Don't Tell Your Story, Someone Else Will," *Forbes*, October 31, 2014, https://www.forbes.com/sites/carminegallo/2014/10/31/if-you-dont-tell-your-story-someone-else-will/.

The task is clear. We need to tell the story of the reign of God—and tell it well. We need to tell the stories of God's activity in creation, the stories of our communities, and our personal stories. We need to give voice to others—to help them tell their stories. The opportunity for us to tell those stories are more ubiquitous than ever, given the many tools and platforms for publishing we have at hand. The challenge is to develop the competencies to use them.

The Church Leader as Digital Communicator

If everyone can publish, perhaps no one can "publish." It follows the same principle that, if everyone speaks at the same time, no one can hear through the din. If everyone is called to tell the story, how does anyone get heard?

Futurist Joel Barker makes the point that a leader is a person you will follow to a place you wouldn't go by yourself. This understanding indicates that leadership is not something that is bestowed as much as it is something that is earned. Many who are called leaders are really managers, which is in and of itself a necessary calling. But real leadership is gauged by the way people *choose* to follow leaders. It is appropriate that social media platforms like Facebook and Twitter use the term "Follow" to click when subscribing to a poster's viewership. What would it take, in the digital world, for people to *choose* to follow you?

Before people can win a Pulitzer Prize, they must learn to write a paragraph. Likewise, before people can master online communication, they must know the kinds of tools available, the features of each tool, and the ways and times for using them. Additionally, tools and platforms can be combined to tell stories more powerfully than ever before.

An online leader is a person people *choose* to follow, subscribe to, seek out, and quote. The characteristics that entice people to follow such leaders are the soft skills of ministry.

In thinking about cultivating a viewership, ministers can ask themselves:

- Why would people choose to follow me?

- What makes me trustworthy?

- Do I have content and stories worth telling?

- Do I have the courage to make my faith story public?

- Do I know where I can find rich stories worthy of passing on?

- Do I have a gift for creating stories?

- Am I familiar with the ways I can deliver the story, online and off?

- Am I willing to live into the story I tell?

- What do I need to make my storytelling easily consumable (readable, easy on the eyes and ears, satisfying to read/watch/hear)?

- What if I have no talent for creating audiovisuals? Do I know someone who does?

- Does a leader need to be an individual? Can leadership be provided by a team—or even a full community? If so, what does this leadership look like?

An Example of an Effective Storyteller

Gerard Thomas Straub was the associate producer of Luke and Laura's wedding on ABC's *General Hospital*, the highest-rated hour in soap opera history. He was wealthy and powerful, and he rubbed shoulders with celebrities. He was raised Roman Catholic, dabbled in the charismatic movement, and worked at Pat Robertson's Christian Broadcasting Network (CBN) for about two-and-a-half years. Gerry struggled with his own faith, identifying primarily as a secular humanist after his experience at CBN. Later, after a conversion experience at a church in Italy, he turned his talent from commercial filmmaking to "Putting the Power of Film at the Service of the Poor" (http://www.paxetbonumcomm.org).

Gerry traveled the world, filming extremely impoverished areas from outcast areas of Brazil to a depressed section of America's own Philadelphia. He would not only tell the stories of deep poverty and misery, but then feature those who followed the call of the Gospel to help as they could in those locations and situations. Gerry would share the stories with churches and organizations through talks and retreats, accompanied by the persuasive music, audio, and visuals of his projected DVDs. It was his personal presence, earnest and soft voice, and humble words that won the trust of many in attendance.

Shortly after Gerry filmed the horrific poverty of Cité Soleil in Haiti, a 2010 earthquake further ravaged the nation. Gerry felt he needed to do something more concrete, and subsequently founded Santa Chiara's Children's Center. As of this writing, the center has fifty-two children staying there, with another eight connecting during the daytime. This is such a drop in the bucket compared to the immense need in Haiti, but that is the point. Gerry was able to take everything he had learned throughout his life, and turn it into what he could do. Sixty kids are served who otherwise would not have been served. Staff have been employed, and hundreds hear the story of Santa Chiara Children's Center through a daily journal sent early each morning without fail—except for the occasional power outage or some other very rare event.

What makes Gerry a great communicator?

- He is a leader. People choose to follow him where they would not otherwise go.

- He has a story to tell, and he tells it convincingly. And, most importantly, it is a compelling story.

- He is trustworthy. He isn't perfect, and he is very up-front about that. He is authentic.

- He isn't widely versed in technology but has chosen a few tools to tell his stories—and mastered them. Gerry knows how to take incredible photos, create deeply moving videos, and write incredible books on spirituality and social concerns. He knows how to use group email to share his story. Additionally, he knows people who are willing to pick up other pieces to expand his readership, like maintaining the Santa Chiara Children's Center website at https://santachiaracc .org/ (which contains an archive of his journal) and Facebook presence at https://www.facebook.com /SantaChiaraCC.

- He is consistently telling the story. This is the type of consistency that helps shape a culture.

Gerry writes in his daily journal,

> I no longer need statistics to tell me how bad things are in Haiti. I have two eyes that inform me every time I leave Santa Chiara. Even during a short, pre-dawn drive to the Missionaries of Charity my green eyes always see things that break my heart.
> My days in Haiti are filled with uncertainty. That is especially true for poor Haitians. A minor crisis tumbles them into despair. Yet, they pick themselves up, find a reason to smile, and keep going. The garbage is piled high. The roads are atrocious. Hunger is omnipresent. Violence is just around the corner. In Haiti, life is precarious and unstable. This is truly exhausting . . . for Haitians and for me.

To learn more about Gerry's gift of storytelling, watch the video of his presentation at Boston College, "From Hollywood to Haiti: A Filmmaker's Journey with the Poor" (https://youtu.be/ED61FaN4oLI).

Begin with the Beauty

Bishop Robert Barron says, "In our postmodern culture, beginning with the true, 'Here's what you should believe,' or the good, 'Here's how you should behave,' is often met with skepticism and defensiveness. So why not try the third of the great transcendentals? The Beautiful!"[3]

If you find yourself dry on ideas for a story, tell of the beauty of your community, the beauty of creation around your church, the beauty of your sanctuary, and indeed, the beauty of the reign of God. It is hard to run out of ideas, and you sidestep a lot of the potential for argument.

Digital Platforms and Tools for Telling the Story

The Christian story needs to be told well, and it needs to be told often in order to reshape and define our culture. To be sure, the Christian story is not a one-time narrative like *Harry Potter* or *Lord of the Rings*. The Christian story is constantly unfolding, especially as we disciples take it on as our own, live into it, become who we want to be, and invite others to join us. The platforms we use can range from websites to postings on social media.

Surely, our personal story includes narratives from the past, stories that have a beginning and an end and that contribute to the larger story of the reign of God. But it also

3. Robert Barron, "Outreach to the Unaffiliated," United States Conference of Catholic Bishops, April 21, 2020, www.usccb.org/committees /evangelization-catechesis/outreach-unaffiliated.

includes current events, feelings, and reactions that are part of our communal story. Our personal story includes desires and struggles and ecstatic moments of joy. It is not enough to simply put stories online: our story needs to be compelling enough to elicit an audience who will want to follow.

The Christian story and our personal stories can be told in a variety of ways. It can be told in a meaningful photo, with or without a text overlay. It can be a long audio podcast or a short song. It can be an action video, a presentation, or a music video with inspirational scenery. It can be told through a combination of media. A photo can deliver a powerful message, but a photo in motion à la Ken Burns with a little elegant text for clarity and inspirational background music for affect can deepen the effectiveness of the photo.

Using storytelling to communicate with your church community helps the information reach members on a personal level. Thanks to the digital era, communicating with members through storytelling is now easier than ever. Stories can be read and shared across a variety of platforms. Digital storytelling is a relationship-building tool that can provide a transparent view into the workings of your church. You tell your story by relating to people on a personal level. Figure out their needs and wants, and use your platforms to engage them.

One of the best forms of communicating with church members is through digital platforms. Most of your congregation has immediate access to web-based content or smartphone apps. This makes spreading information quick and easy. By sharing information through a storytelling format, you can better engage and connect with your congregation. Leaders need to be familiar with the several essential tools so they may choose the most appropriate ones for their audience and their own skill set, including websites, blogs, social media platforms, interaction and feedback tools, communication tools, online learning platforms, and media creation tools. Each tool is described below. For complete information and website links for each tool, go to the Resource at the end of the chapter. Remember that any listing of technology tools may be outdated or discontinued as things change so quickly. Simply search "tools like 'tool name'" for alternatives.

1. Websites

A church website or a stand-alone faith formation (or other ministry) website provides a hub for communication, connection, and formation. Service and programming times, bulletins, staff information, event announcements, mission statements, and all sorts of multimedia content can be hosted there. The location is static, but the content is continually updated. People usually visit a website (read: they come to us) for a specific purpose. It is not necessarily the best tool for outreach, but once people arrive, the story we tell can be formative. Everything posted on a website should be done with this question in mind: What story is this item telling and to whom?

A church website needs to address two different audiences: church members and first-time guests. The home page should be invitational and appealing to first-time users by providing answers to questions they might ask about the church. Make it easy to find information for members and first-time guests. Present your church culture, style, and practices. Provide information on worship and ministries, as well as contact information for staff and directions to the church or gatherings.

Remember that design matters. The website needs to look attractive and inviting. Use white space to create visual separation between elements and help viewers quickly see breaks, which help you tell the website visitor what's most important to look at. Photography influences everything. Your website needs to have real pictures of real people. It needs to show people what your community is like (so no pictures of empty churches!).

Here are several suggestions for web usability from Steve Krug's excellent and easy-to-use book *Don't Make Me Think: A Common Sense Approach to Web Usability*[4]:

1. Don't make the user think—make web pages self-explanatory so the user hardly has any perceived effort to understand them, for example, clear choice of labels, clearly "clickable" items, terms that are simple to search.

2. People generally don't read web pages closely; they scan, so design for scanning rather than reading.

3. Create a clear visual hierarchy and menu system (main menu, submenus).

4. Make it very clear how to navigate the site, with clear "signposts" on all pages.

5. Omit needless words.

6. The home page needs the greatest design care to convey site identity and mission.

7. Promote user goodwill by making the typical tasks easy to do and easy to recover from errors. Avoid anything likely to irritate users.

Here are four suggestions for website design from Robin Williams's book, *The Non-Designer's Design Book*: *Proximity, Alignment, Repetition,* and *Contrast*.[5]

> *Proximity*: Items relating to each other should be grouped closely together. When several items are in

---

4. Steve Krug, *Don't Make Me Think: A Common Sense Approach to Web Usability*, 3rd ed. (Berkeley: New Riders, 2014).
5. Robin Williams, *The Non-Designer's Design Book*, 4th ed. (San Francisco: Peachpit Press, 2014).

close proximity, they become one visual unit rather than several separate units. This helps organize information, reduces clutter, and gives the reader a clear structure. You should be asking yourself constantly: Can you find everything you need on your page easily? What is it that people will take note of?

Alignment: Nothing should be placed on the page arbitrarily. Every element should have some visual connection with the other element on the page. When items are aligned on the page, we see a strong cohesive unit. . . . Even when aligned items are physically separated from each other, there is an invisible line that connects them. The principle of alignment tells the reader that even though these items are not close, they belong to the same piece. You should be asking yourself constantly: Does everything line up or have I got things centered, left-aligned, or out of place?

Repetition: Repeating visual elements of the design throughout the piece by means of color, shape, spatial relationship, line thickness, font, size, graphic concept, etc. This helps to organize the piece and strengthen unity. By repeating design elements on the screen such as titles, layout, color schemes and so on, you provide visual cues to your reader so that they're able to follow the content and understand how it all fits together.

Contrast: If items do not belong to the same unit, then make them very different. Contrast is often the most important visual attraction on a page—it's what makes the reader look at the page in the first place. Contrast has two purposes that are inextricable from each other. One purpose is to create a point of interest on the page. If a page is interesting to look at, it is more likely to be read. The other purpose is to organize information. A reader should be able to instantly understand the way the information is organized—the logical flow from one item to another. Contrasting items should never confuse readers or create a focus on something that is not supposed to be a focus.

By applying a little contrast in the right places, you can avoid elements on the page that are merely similar: making different things different, making the important elements stand out, muting less important elements, and creating a bit of dynamism on the screen.

Here are a some of the screen elements that you should look at providing contrast to: sizes, colors, fonts, line thickness, location of blocks or elements on the screen (e.g., text blocks), spacing between elements, and shapes. Titles, body text, bold text, and underlining help to organize information, make it meaningful and memorable, and provide direction or instruction for your learners.[6]

Tools to Explore. Weebly, Wix, GoDaddy, and Google Sites are examples of website builders who will also host your website. WordPress is a more advanced platform on which you can build a website using hundreds of ready-made templates. Many Christian publishers (bulletins, hymnals) also provide web creation and hosting services.

The easiest way to develop or enhance your website is by reviewing church websites that use good design and present their content (story) in engaging ways. Check out the examples in the Resource at the end of the chapter.

2. Blogs

Blogs are collections of posts—ideal for online journaling—to share experiences and observations as a leader. Blogs can be used to deliver narratives, articles, editorials, lessons, and more genres. Usually, blog posts are written with

6. Adapted from Zhenghui Shen, "Robin Williams' Four Basic Design Principles for Non-Designers," Wiredcraft, April 16, 2019, https://wiredcraft .com/blog/robin-williams-four-basic-design-principles-for-non-designers.

some regularity on a specific theme or topic from a person's unique point of view. They can also be written on different topics and then categorized, automatically organizing themselves. A characteristic of blogs is that a new article or post appears in the same spot as the previous post, pushing it out of the limelight while not deleting it. A website would be structured to house a larger variety of information and therefore be designed for easy, dependable navigation, for the browsing comfort of frequent visitors. A blog can often be found at the same page on a larger website. For blog posts, comments can provide for some level of discussion, although they can also be turned off to make a conversation board into a sounding board. It can be set up so viewers can subscribe to be notified when a new post appears. Blogs can be public or private.

A blog can be from one person, such as "From the Desk of Our Pastor," or from a team, like "Church Staff Musings." It is even possible to set up a secret email address so people can post to the blog remotely, even including a photo, by sending an email to that address. Some organizations have made a private blog into a book club or adult faith formation environment with comments allowing for simple interaction.

Here are several important guidelines for writing a blog:

1. Understand your audience: What do they want to know? What will they resonate with?

2. Create your blog domain. The blogging platform you select will help you set up a domain.

3. Customize your blog's theme to reflect the content you will be presenting.

4. Develop a title and outline for your blog post.

5. Create a catchy title.

6. Write an introduction (and make it compelling).

7. Organize your content using the outline.

8. Write your post.

9. Proofread and edit your post.

10. Design your visual appearance. Add a photo and images to the design.

11. Insert a CTA (call to action) at the end of the post indicating what you would like the reader to do.

Tools to Explore. WordPress and Blogger provide blogging platforms. Website builders Wix and Weebly also include a blogging platform. Check out several examples of blogs, targeted to different audiences with difference designs, that you can review for design ideas as you create your own blog.

3. Social Media Platforms

A website can be like a large, rich garden of information and stories about a community that stays in the same easy-to-find location. Social media platforms (Facebook, Instagram, Twitter, Pinterest, TikTok) are like seeds being scattered in all directions, each post, easily shareable, containing a glimpse of the larger story. People are on social media. We need to tell our story where people are.

Social media items are meant to be short and frequent, each being easy to consume and meant to keep a community's story ever fresh in the public's eye. The power of social media is that it can capture the attention of a wide community and then drive readers back to a congregation's website or blog for further information. Think of social media as outreach, going out to people, whereas a website is the home base dependent upon people coming to it. Many organizations post news or informational headlines on social media which link back to their home page.

Conceptually, a website is a bulletin board of information, whereas social media is an ongoing conversation. Social media are the seeds throughout the cyberworld which, by nature, continue to shape the culture of the church community. Since social media is a stage for attracting attention, it is a place where photos and graphics can tell short, effective stories with few or no words. Memes that go viral are examples of graphics supporting a larger story.

Here are several important things to remember as you design social media platforms.

1. The social media platform needs to reflect the life of your community in posts, photos, and videos.

2. A moderator is needed to regularly engage with people participating in a particular social media platform. This is hospitality—watching, reading, responding, and interacting.

3. Social media needs to be monitored constantly. Unfortunately, comments can be negative and even cruel. Be clear about your rules of engagement and state that hostility will not be tolerated. When necessary, delete posts and even block people from posting. This is a time to tell the story of God's love and how we are called to live faithfully.

4. One well-done post, graphic, or video is better than five hastily created posts. We want to present our story with the elegance it deserves.

5. There are wonderful people on social media who you will want to share with your church. Since you have no control over what they may post, use caution in recommending authors on your official pages and groups.

6. One of the advantages of posting in social media and on your blog is that you can schedule publishing times

in advance. You can create multiple posts and schedule them to appear at different times.

7. We need to be careful with stories and photos or videos
of children on social media. Be sure to follow church
protocols for publishing stories, such as refraining
from publishing faces connected with identifying
information.

Tools to Explore. Facebook, Twitter, Instagram, Pinterest, and
TikTok are five of the largest and most popular social media
platforms to use. They allow you to post text, photos, videos, and links to other online places and resources. There are
many similarities among each platform in the dynamics of
posting, commenting, replying, and sharing of posts. Each
platform has a special niche and audience(s). Check out the
articles describing churches that have robust social media
using a variety of platforms (Facebook, Twitter, Instagram).

4. Feedback Tools

Despite the comment features built into websites, blogs, and
social media, they are designed more for broadcasting (us
talking) than listening. It is important for our online presence
to provide ways in which we can hear from our visitors.

The conversational attributes of social media can provide
effective ways for congregations to listen to their members. There are also online survey tools that can ask specific
questions so that we obtain focused answers. Online forms,
like SurveyMonkey and Google Forms, can be used for assessment, evaluation, and program registration. The main
advantage of such tools is that the answers can be compiled
into a Microsoft Excel or Google Sheets compatible file for
easy analysis.

Once you become familiar with the survey or form tool of
your choice, you can become quite creative. You can embed
your created forms into a blog or web page. You can use

these tools for a variety of purposes: to gather feedback on new projects, invite people to sign up for ministries, conduct a gifts and talents campaign, obtain thoughts on a new building project, evaluate church ministries and programming, and much more. If constructed properly, a form can give people chance to create and/or tell their story!

Tools to Explore. Google Forms, SurveyMonkey, and Padlet provide three tools for obtaining feedback and listening to people. Many website builders have incorporated forms into their features, and these forms can be customized for a number of purposes.

5. Direct Communication
When you need to send a message or new newsletter efficiently, you can use a number of email and text services designed to make the job easy. While this may not seem to be storytelling in the classical sense, it can build up and shape the culture of a community and form people's faith.

Email services can be used to send a weekly newsletter (church bulletin) to church members, program announcements to specific audiences, faith formation content (such as weekly Advent or Lent reflections activities), and much more. Direct communication via email or text can include prayer requests, ministry updates, worship service details, volunteer opportunities, sermons and Sunday worship activities, event registration details, a Bible reading plan, prayers for the week, and much more. Using an email service allows you to create mailing lists for difference audiences with targeted content. It also provides a way to get feedback on open rates for each mailing.

Tools to Explore. Flocknote, Mailchimp, and Constant Contact are three services that provide email services. Flocknote also has a texting feature. Remind and GroupMe provide group texting ability.

6. Online Learning Platforms

If you take each of the individual tools, with their own strengths, and put them together in an online environment secure enough for open sharing, community building, and even learning assessment, you'd have a powerful way to tell your story, listen to others share their stories, help others tell their stories, and process the larger story of Christian salvation together. Learning Management Systems (LMS) provide such functionality.

In an LMS, content can be delivered in an organized fashion in a class-like environment. Students of all ages may have an account (those under 13 need parental involvement, so their activities can be tracked and assessed if desired). A main advantage of an LMS is that classes can be set up to include lessons with multimedia and text-based content, discussion forums, chat rooms, live video conferencing and more. It is a way to dig deeply into aspects of our stories over a span of weeks. Adults can find a safe place to hold online Bible studies and book reads within an LMS.

Tools to Explore. Schoology, Edmodo, Seesaw, and Google Classroom are four examples of online learning platforms.

7. Media Creation Resources and Tools for Pictures/ Photos, Audio, Video Clips, and Text

Church leaders do not need to be media producers, but they should know enough about the tools to imagine ways of telling the story. What follows is a brief survey of media tools for your ministry.

Pictures and Photos

In and of itself, a picture or photo can tell an effective story. It can quickly convey a message as people scroll through Facebook feeds or provide small Christian communities a focal point during shared *visio divina* prayer. Of course, you can draw your own pictures or take your own photos to avoid copyright issues, or you can ask for permission to use original photos from your community taken at events, ministries, and even travels.

Tools to Explore. Pixabay, Unsplash, and Pexels provide free photo libraries that you can use without copyright restrictions.

If you choose to create your own graphics, enhance photos to add some added emotional impact, or add text to your photos, you can use Canva, Adobe Creative Cloud Express (formerly Adobe Spark), SuperImpose, and presentation programs PowerPoint and Keynote (where slides can be exported as images). For animated GIFs there is Giphy and Werble.

Recording or Downloading Audio
It is said that mistakes with photography and video are easily forgivable, but not so with audio. It is imperative to get the mood right on videos with appropriate music. Barely intelligible narration is almost worse than no narration at all. You need clean and moving music to enhance your videos, and, if you are recording your own music or voice-overs, you need solid recording software and a good microphone. Thankfully, the quality of microphones in computers and smartphones is improving, so make sure you test yours before investing in an external one.

Tools to Explore. Adobe Creative Cloud Express (formerly Adobe Spark), Garageband (Apple), Audacity, and your own smartphone applications provide ways to record audio. YouTube's Audio Library in the YouTube Studio provides music that is copyright friendly.

Clips
Short video clips can go a long way in enhancing a video creation. For example, as you create a slide show with Adobe Creative Cloud Express, you can add motion to a slide by inserting a clip of a waterfall or snowstorm.

Tools to Explore. Pixabay and Pexels offer video clips for free. Intro Designer is an app for designing video clips. PowerPoint and Keynote allow you to save a presentation as a video and add audio.

Video

Once you are comfortable taking photos with your smartphone, adding some text on top of it, creating stylistic quotes from Scripture or wise people, or even capturing your own video clips, you are ready to move into intentional video creation and editing. While there are a number of tools to explore, many are quite expensive and have a steep learning curve. However, several are free.

When you finish your video and need to send it to someone to view, edit, or post, you will find that the file size is often too large to text or email. Explore online sharing spaces, such as Dropbox, Google Drive, or iCloud. You can upload your video file to these cloud drives, enable sharing, and send the link rather than the file to your recipient. They access and download the video by clicking on the link you send them.

Tools to Explore. Adobe Creative Cloud Express (formerly Adobe Spark), iMovie (Apple), Photos (Windows 10), Animoto, and PowToon provide easy-to-use tools to create videos.

Conclusion

One does not need to be a master of all the tools mentioned above, but a general familiarity with them is invaluable so that you can match the right tools with the purposes of your storytelling. Determine the story you want to create and share, then find the right tool(s) to help you communicate the story to your audience. Stories teach us who we are and who we want to be. They can inspire your community to action.

Resource. Examples of Digital Platforms and Tools for Telling the Story

Website Examples

The easiest way to develop or enhance your website is by reviewing church websites that use good design and present their content (story) in engaging ways. Here are a few good examples to review:

- All Saints Episcopal Church: https://allsaintsatlanta.org

- Bethany Christian Reformed Church: https://www.bethanycrc.org

- Church of the Presentation: https://www.churchofpresentation.org

- Ginghamsburg Church: https://ginghamsburg.org

- GLIDE Church: https://www.glide.org

- Menlo Church: https://menlo.church/home

- Mosaic Church: https://www.mosaicva.com

- Prince of Peace Lutheran Church: https://popmn.org

- St. Anthony on the Lake Catholic Parish: https://www.stanthony.cc

- St. Bartholomew Anglican Church: https://www.stbarts.net.au

- St. Charles Catholic Parish: https://www.stcharlespdx.org

Blog Examples

Here are a few examples of blogs, targeted to different audiences with difference designs, that you can review for design ideas as you create your own blog.

- Catechists Journey (Joe Paprocki): https://catechists journey.loyolapress.com

- Family Fire blog (Reframe Ministries): https://family fire.com

- Ginghamsburg Church blog: https://ginghamsburg .org/about-us/church-blog/

- Live Not Lukewarm blog (Deanna Bartalini): https:// livenotlukewarm.com/blog

- Mothering Spirit blog (Laura Kelly Fanucci): https:// motheringspirit.com

- Parent Cue blog (Orange): https://theparentcue.org

- Treasure Box Tuesday (Traci Smith, Family+Faith +Spirit): https://traci-smith.com

- Word on Fire blog: https://www.wordonfire.org /resources/blog

Social Media Examples

Check out the articles describing churches that have robust social media using a variety of platforms (Facebook, Twitter, Instagram).

- Thirty Churches to Follow for Social Media Inspiration: https://www.thecreativepastor.com/thirty -churches-to-follow-for-social-media-inspiration

- Best Churches to Watch on Social Media: https:// prochurchtools.com/the-best-churches-to-follow-on -social-media-in-2020

- The Ultimate Social Media Blueprint for Churches: https://prochurchtools.com/playlist/social-media

- Church Tech Today: https://churchtechtoday.com /topic/churchcomm/churchsocial

Resource. A Digital Audit

A useful exercise is to complete a "digital audit" of your church life and ministries. The goal is to describe how your church is currently engaged in digitally integrated ministry. Use the following questions to structure your inventory.

Church Website

- How does your church website serve as a hub for community information?

- How does your church website welcome new people into the faith community?

- How does your church website provide faith-forming content and activities for all ages?

Social Media

- Which social media platforms does your church use to communicate and connect with people (e.g., Facebook, Instagram, Twitter, Pinterest, TikTok)?

- Who are you trying to reach with each social media platform?

- What does your church communicate through social media?

- How does your church connect people through social media?

Communication and Connecting

- How does your church communicate using digital tools?

- What kinds of content or information does your church communicate?

- How does your church communicate through email about church life and activities?

- How does your church utilize texting?

- How does your church use video conferencing for meetings and leadership teams?

Ministries

- How does your church provide online access to content from at-church ministries and programs, such as Sunday sermons, presentations, classes, and more?

- How does your church provide online content for Advent and Christmas, Lent, Holy Week, Easter, and other seasons and church events?

- How does your church provide online programming for families, adolescents, and adults, such as online courses, book group, prayer group, topical discussion, Bible study, and more?

- How do church ministries utilize streaming and video conferencing technologies?

Church Community

Identify how each of the six seasons of the life cycle use digital tools and media: children (0–10) and their parents, adolescents (11–19), young adults (20s–30s), midlife adults (40s–50s), mature adults (60s–70s), and older adults (80+). Consider the following:

- Which digital technologies do they use (computers, tablets, phones)?

- What is the quality of their internet connection at home and the speed of their cell phone service?

- What do they go online to do (read, connect, create, watch, listen)?

- Which social media platforms do they utilize?

Resource. A Guide to Digital Platforms and Tools

Websites

One of the easiest tools to create an online presence is a website builder. Searching "free website builders" will point you in the right direction to explore options to create your online hub quickly and comparatively easily. Four good options are *Weebly* (https://www.weebly.com), *Wix* (https://www.wix.com), *GoDaddy* (https://www.godaddy.com), and *Google Sites* (https://sites.google.com). The services offer a free account and will host your website and provide a free sub-domain name that includes the hosting company's name, like "yoursite.webhostname.com." There are tutorials available on YouTube. The first three services have paid options that remove their advertising, offer a free unique domain name for the first year, and provide more robust features.

WordPress (Wordpress.org) is actually free software that runs a blog or website. You buy space on a server somewhere in cyberspace and either install WordPress yourself or have the server company take care of it for you. Often, your account will include an easy installation feature. *WordPress* is not as easy to use as site builders (although it is getting there), but because of the large user base, it offers a lot of power and control. As of this writing, over 40 percent of websites on the internet run on WordPress. Note: Wordpress.com (not .org) is a service that provides a quick, easy way to get a WordPress-based site going, but it is really optimized for blogging more so than a full website. It, too, has a free option.

Blogs

WordPress (https://wordpress.com) for hosting and https://wordpress.org to download the software for installation on a server service like Bluehost.com or Hostgator.com. WordPress was created for blogging, but its power and popularity made the software a perfect tool for developing websites as well.

Blogger (https://www.blogger.com) is a Google tool. It is free, simple, and optimized for blogging. It formats itself for blogging, which is good, but thus it isn't appropriate for website development. It is easy to make public or to make more secure if you want to use it for such things as a private book club or maybe for a closed group.

Social Media Platforms

Facebook Pages (https://facebook.com) can be thought of as mini-websites, homes for your organization on Facebook. Posts contain text, graphics, stories, and videos. Livestreaming can be offered on Facebook, with a scrolling comment area for participants to interact. Facebook Groups allow people with similar interests to "gather" online asynchronously and share ideas and explore questions. Messenger rooms are video chat environments where more than one person can join in a session, similar to Zoom.

Twitter (https://twitter.com) is built on the premise that short is best. It allows for short texts and photos. But you can also "tweet" links to websites with longer posts.

Instagram (https://instagram.com) has placed its emphasis on photos, stories, and short videos. It can be integrated with Facebook, who owns it, to have a post appear both places.

Pinterest (https://pinterest.com) is an image-hosting and -sharing platform designed for projects, which it calls "boards." Think of Pinterest as a virtual pinboard or bulletin board but with organizational and bookmarking tools. Saving and sharing your Pinterest ideas is centered around boards, with each image dubbed a "pin." You can create a board for just about anything and pin any picture to that board.

TikTok (https://tiktok.com) is a platform where you can upload videos up to three minutes in length (as of this writing). Algorithms feed them to people who view similar topics to your content. It would be interesting for youth and young adult groups to experiment with TikTok as a tool for evangelization. Video memes would work well here.

Video Conferencing and Streaming

Zoom (https://zoom.us) provides an easy, reliable cloud platform for video and audio conferencing, collaboration, chat, and webinars across mobile devices, desktops, telephones, and room systems. You can use Zoom to livestream worship, programs, presentations, etc. You can use Zoom to organize online interactive classes, small group studies (online Bible study), and much more.

Microsoft Teams (https://www.microsoft.com/en-us/microsoft-teams/group-chat-software) and *Google Meet* (https://meet.google.com) provide many similar features.

Facebook Live (https://www.facebook.com/formedia/solutions/facebook-live) and *YouTube Live* (https://www.youtube.com/howyoutubeworks/product-features/live) provide excellent ways to livestream worship, events, and presentations. Every platform allows you to record the event for future use.

Feedback and Registration

Google Forms (https://www.google.com/forms/about/) is a free electronic-form-building tool. You supply the questions or other fields for data gathering, and visitors fill in the fields through their web browsers. The data is compiled into a Microsoft Excel or Google Sheets compatible file that can be analyzed and shared quite securely.

SurveyMonkey (https://surveymonkey.com) is a complete survey service with annual fees. In addition to using SurveyMonkey for surveys and evaluations, you can connect a SurveyMonkey form for program registration to a Stripe account to collect money for registration fees, books, tickets, donations, and much more.

Padlet (https://padlet.com) is a graphically based bulletin board tool that can look just like a classroom bulletin board. Visitors can double-click anywhere and post text, video links, files, photos, and URLs of other web locations. Anyone watching the bulletin board will see the post appear, and they can reply through the comment field in the post or create their own new post. Padlet is great for an asynchronous brainstorming session, sharing of websites, writing reflections on chapters of a book read, telling stories of forgiveness, listing things we are grateful for, and more.

Online Learning Platform (Learning Management System)

An online "classroom" provides an environment for sharing content, texts, videos, projects, and assignments with people online. It is an environment where teachers/leaders can guide learning and where they can interact with participants in a safe space. A learning platform is essential for online-only and blended models of faith formation. *Edmodo* (https://new.edmodo.com), *Seesaw* (https://web.seesaw.me), and *Google Classroom* (https://edu.google.com) provide free platforms for individual teachers/leaders and classes.

Facebook Groups (https://www.facebook.com/help/1629740080681586) provides an interactive environment for online programs and blended programs that you can add to all programming. You can organize groups for adults to discuss the Sunday Scripture readings or to share insights from an online Bible study or theology course. You can organize groups for parents to share their family experiences with the Bible story of the week or prayer practice.

Microsoft Teams (https://www.microsoft.com/en-us
/microsoft-teams/education) is worth exploring for online
learning, especially if you use Microsoft products regularly.

Direct Communication

Remind (https://remind.com) is a service that allows you to
send a note out to a community or a subset of a community.
Your note is delivered as a text message or email, depend-
ing on how members elect to receive it. You can even send
photos/graphics or links to files. Of course, you will want
to follow rules of communication etiquette to avoid inun-
dating people . . . but it can be a very powerful tool for the
right group in the right situation. One such idea would be
sending out short daily reflections to a group of interested
people during Lent who submitted their phone numbers or
email addresses using Google Forms.

Flocknote (https://flocknote.com) is used by many churches
to deliver texts and emails and to organize replies. You can
add RSVP features, survey questions, graphics, and more.

Mailchimp (https://mailchimp.com) and *Constant Contact*
(https://constantcontact.com) are two emailing services for
sending out a "blast" of emails. These messages can be quite
attractive, using templates supplied by their company. Both
companies work hard to make sure that their emails don't
wind up in someone's spam folder. Mailchimp offers a free
account with up to two thousand contacts in one audience.
A congregation would be considered an audience, and you
can tag and group contacts within that audience for targeting specific sets of people.

Texting: Use texting to send reminders, links to activities
on the faith formation website, and short activities (prayer,
Bible verse, etc.). There are a variety of free texting apps that
you can use with iOS and Android. Check out GroupMe—
app and web-based interface (https://groupme.com/en

-US), Telegram—app and web-based interface (https://
telegram.org), WhatsApp (https://www.whatsapp.com),
and Viber (https://www.viber.com).

Photos

Canva (https://www.canva.com) is an all-around graphic
design tool. You don't draw pictures per se, but you can
add photos and pre-designed elements to create graphics,
as well as posters, flyers, Facebook and Instagram posts,
videos with audio, and more. The free account is a good
place to start for creating memes (text on graphics) or styl-
izing a text announcement or video title. A limited free account is available.

Adobe Creative Cloud Express (https://www.adobe.com
/express/) offers designers easy ways of creating videos
(slide shows with audio and video clips), single web pages,
and other graphics as Canva above.

SuperImpose X (http://www.superimposeapp.com) enhances graphics on a mobile device, with more advanced
capabilities such as masking, blending, and opacity control.

Animated GIFs

Giphy (https://giphy.com) allows you to browse GIFs, or
moving pictures, made by others, and create your own to
attract attention to your very, very short story.

Werble (https://www.werbleapp.com) gives you the ability
to add your photos and enhance them with moving effects,
like rolling waves, moving skies, moving angel wings, fire-
works, and more. You can save your creations as GIFs or
video clips.

Audio

YouTube's Audio Library is a collection of copyright friendly
music, searchable by genre, to add to your videos as intro,

outro, or background music. You need to create a free *Google* account, which gives you access to *YouTube Studio*. Log in to the studio dashboard at https://studio.youtube.com, and find the audio library in the left-hand menu. You will be taken to the list of music to search, sample, and download.

Adobe Creative Cloud Express (https://www.adobe.com /express/) provides background music to choose while creating a slide show on their site. It also allows you to record slide narration over any and all slides you choose. Additionally, you can upload your own music files.

Garageband, free with an Apple device, is a multitrack re- cording studio for recording and mixing voice and music. It also contains many loops in various music genres and in- struments to create your own music for video and podcasts.

Audacity (https://www.audacityteam.org) is worth spending the time to learn (see YouTube videos). It is a powerful re- cording application that is not pretty—but pretty easy to use after you learn to ignore the many features you don't need.

Video
Adobe Creative Cloud Express (https://www.adobe.com/ex- press/create/video) is a great place to start if you've never created a video before. Create a free Adobe account, and then follow their prompts to create a wonderful slide show with your photos or those that they provide, and overlay text, add music, and even record narrative right through your internet browser. They even supply credits at the end for media to use from their collection. Then, you download the video for viewing, sharing, or uploading to YouTube so you can embed it easily in social media.

iMovie, free with an Apple device, is very easy to use and comes with a robust set of features. Searching YouTube for tutorials is a great way to learn this app.

Photos, free with Microsoft Windows 10, should be named "Photos and Videos" because it comes with an editing environment to create a video using the photos and video clips you have on your computer.

Powtoon (https://www.powtoon.com) and *Animoto* (https://animoto.com) are just two examples of online video creation tools that offer attractive templates and some robust features for free. Learning them is fun and expands your knowledge of different video interfaces for future exploration of the many video creation tools offered online.

Video Clips

Pixabay (https://pixabay.com) and *Pexels* (https://pexels.com) are sites that offer free photos as mentioned above and also offer video clips for free. Clips of fire, starry skies, children playing, etc., can add an important mood to your slide show or video.

Intro Designer (www.introdesignerapp.com) is an iOS app for designing striking intro clips that allow you to add text and manage the visual styles of the media offered. You can then save your work to add to your video creation.

CHAPTER THREE

Community and Relationship Building in Virtual Spaces

Deanna Bartalini and Claudia McIvor

It is safe to say that human beings are meant for community. We are among the creatures of the earth considered to be social beings—along with everything from ants to wolves. Aristotle declared that man is by nature a social animal. This is a belief that is echoed through the ages by philosophers, religious leaders, and scientists alike. Our social nature is patterned by our trinitarian God; or rather, our human nature is reflective of God's trinitarian nature. We are made for community and for communion. Wherever and however we meet, it is for and about relationship and community in and through Christ. There will be sharing of knowledge, yes. There will be different purposes for gathering, yes. But in the end, we are building up a community of *Christian* believers.

In a gathered time and space, it is perfectly apparent that we tell our stories, share meals, have conversations, worship together, pray together, serve others, and much more. These are the things that Christians have done from the earliest days of the church.

We have had millions of years to adapt to person-to-person socialization and thousands of years to practice

47

in-person Christian community. But in the space of a few short years, a new venue for community has arisen, and the rules and expectations for how and when we gather have changed unexpectedly and quite drastically. The first cell phone was created in 1973. In 2019, more than half of the five billion mobile devices owned were smartphones. More than half of the world's population is using an internet-connected device that was created less than fifty years earlier.[1] Virtual space is not just a concept; it is a reality—an actual place of communication and a vehicle for community and relationship. This new space has the potential for fostering and maintaining healthy Christian relationships.

Desired Traits of Community Online

While digital technologies have changed over the past two decades, one thing that has not changed is what people are looking for when they go online to experience Christian community or church. Researcher, professor, and author Heidi Campbell conducted five years of online and offline interviews and participant observation of people's communication practices in three different online Christian communities with members in North America and the United Kingdom. She found that people most valued six traits about their online communities.

> First, they are looking for a sense of relationship—not simply a place to share information, but a space that allowed them to form a network of social relations and friendships. As a woman from Illinois I interviewed

1. Laura Silver, "Smartphone Ownership Is Growing Rapidly Around the World, but Not Always Equally," *Pew Research Center Global Attitudes and Trends,* February 5, 2019, https://www.pewresearch.org/global/2019/02/05/smartphone-ownership-is-growing-rapidly-around-the-world-but-not-always-equally.

said, "What I am experiencing on the internet is a true Christian relationship . . . it makes the whole thing of the Bride of Christ more feasible, a reality . . . not just something to read about."

Second, they are looking for care, a space where they can give and receive support and encouragement. As a lawyer from Michigan I spoke to reported, "I've had communication online where I've really felt 'hugged' when I really need it."

Third, they are looking for value, to be appreciated for their contributions and presence online. A man from the UK involved in an online Anglican community described this saying, "I've tried to leave the group three times, but I've always rejoined because I miss the people, I miss the banter, and I miss how they encourage me."

Fourth, people are longing for connection, the ability to have 24-7 contact with others that internet technology easily facilitates. An accountant from Missouri involved in a prophetic learning community explained, "I know on the (group) when someone says they'll pray for me, they will. That's a trust because I have seen it happen. Whereas at church someone can say, 'Oh, I'll pray for you,' but I don't know that they will."

Fifth, people online are looking for intimate communication—a safe place where they can be themselves and communicate openly with others. "We have been absolutely amazed at how the Holy Spirit can use something like email to touch the hearts of folks halfway around the world, even to the point that they weep," said a vision-impaired woman from the UK who described the online Christian group as her church.

The sixth and final component, people in online communities long for fellowship with others of a shared faith, like-minded believers who share their beliefs and sense of purpose. As a man from Toronto reported, "The (group) is just another expression of

Jesus Christ and his church and his calling of us to be ministers of the gospel."[2]

The research makes clear that people are looking for a faith-based social network where they can build relationships, share their faith, and find meaning and value in their interactions and place in the groups. As Campbell notes, "Over and over, I hear these same traits echoed in interviews of what people value most about the relationships and communities they are invested in, both online and offline."[3]

Building Christian Community in Virtual Spaces

The purpose of forming relationships and building Christian community in virtual space is the creation and support of human relationships. Pope Benedict XVI writes,

> While the speed with which the new technologies have evolved in terms of their efficiency and reliability is rightly a source of wonder, their popularity with users should not surprise us, as they respond to a fundamental desire of people to communicate and to relate to each other. This desire for communication and friendship is rooted in our very nature as human beings and cannot be adequately understood as a response to technical innovations. In the light of the biblical message, it should be seen primarily as a reflection of our participation in the communicative and unifying Love of God, who desires to make of all humanity one family. When we find ourselves drawn towards other people, when we want to know more about them and make ourselves known to them, we are responding to God's

2. Heidi Campbell, "What Religious Groups Need to Consider When Trying to Do Church Online," in *The Distanced Church: Reflections on Doing Church Online*, ed. Heidi A. Campbell, 50 (Digital Religion Publications, 2020), https://oaktrust.library.tamu.edu/handle/1969.1/187970.

3. Campbell, "What Religious Groups Need to Consider," 50.

call—a call that is imprinted in our nature as beings created in the image and likeness of God, the God of communication and communion.[4]

When we think about the nature of a Christian community—gathered in a physical space or in a virtual space, it is important to remember that we are following a God who promises to make all things new, to bring life from death, and to make God's people a community of faith, hope, and love. The Acts of the Apostles tells us how the early Christian communities gathered and what their earliest actions were.

> All who believed were together and had all things in common; they would sell their possessions and goods and distribute the proceeds to all, as any had need. Day by day, as they spent much time together in the temple, they broke bread at home and ate their food with glad and generous hearts, praising God and having the goodwill of all the people. And day by day the Lord added to their number those who were being saved. (Acts 2:44-47, NRSV)

> Now the whole group of those who believed were of one heart and soul, and no one claimed private ownership of any possessions, but everything they owned was held in common. With great power the apostles gave their testimony to the resurrection of the Lord Jesus, and great grace was upon them all. There was not a needy person among them, for as many as owned lands or houses sold them and brought the proceeds of what was sold. (Acts 4:32-34, NRSV)

4. Pope Benedict XVI, "New Technologies, New Relationships. Promoting a Culture of Respect, Dialogue and Friendship," Message of the Holy Father Benedict XVI for the 43rd World Communications Day, May 24, 2009, http://www.vatican.va/content/benedict-xvi/en/messages/communications/documents/hf_ben-xvi_mes_20090124_43rd-world-communications-day.html.

If we take our model from the earliest Christian communities, Christian community in virtual spaces need to be centered on Christ, be generous, be of service to the community, and be evangelical. It needs to willingly sacrifice for those in need, bring healing to others, proclaim the Gospel, pray and worship God, and welcome others.

Healthy online relationships and communities allow members to be vulnerable and open without transgressing safety boundaries. They are filled with faith, prayers, and expressions and symbols of faith. They provide support and encouragement for living the Christian life—not just online but in all areas of life. They incorporate prayer and celebration. They are supported by members who have the expertise to create the websites, social media accounts, and online conferencing to support the online community. They are mission-driven, keeping evangelization as the key underpinning of why we are in this virtual space.

The community we seek to develop in virtual spaces is an extension of the Body of Christ into this new human experience of online community. In virtual spaces, we can engage in faith relationships with others. We can share our personal faith journeys. We can pray with and for one another. We can advocate for justice. We can educate and evangelize. In virtual spaces we can be disciples and invite others into discipleship. We can construct virtual spaces that can create and sustain healthy Christian communities.

There are four essential practices for life and ministry in digital spaces. "These basic practices allow people of faith to enter digital communities from a networked, relational, incarnational perspective, with the goal of getting to know others in a more sustained way over time and connecting more deeply within and across communities."[5]

---

5. Keith Anderson and Elizabeth Drescher, *Click2Save Reboot: The Digital Ministry Bible* (New York: Church Publishing, 2018), 150.

The LACE model, developed by Elizabeth Drescher, is a good starting point for nurturing meaningful relationships in the digitally integrated world: *Listen, Attend, Connect,* and *Engage.*

- **L**istening: Taking time to get to know people in social networks based on what they share in profiles, posts, tweets, and so on, rather than making communicating your message the priority

- **A**ttending: Noticing and being present to the experiences and interests of others as they share themselves in digital spaces

- **C**onnecting: Reaching out to others in diverse communities in order to deepen and extend the networks that influence your digital spiritual practice

- **E**ngaging: Building relationships by sharing content, collaborating, and connecting people to others[6]

Ideas for Building Community in Online Settings

There are many ways to build community in online settings. One of the best examples is CaringBridge (www.caringbridge.org), which is dedicated to building a world where no one goes through a health journey alone. A health journey of any kind—diagnosis, injury, illness, pregnancy complications, or other experiences—can be difficult to endure alone. Too often, patients and caregivers feel isolated at a time when support matters most. In these moments, there's no match for the power of community, because healing happens when we're surrounded by our loved ones. CaringBridge has made it simple and safe to offer or ask for support when it's needed most. More than three

6. Anderson and Drescher, *Click2Save*, 149–50.

hundred thousand people use their private and ad-free platform every single day, sharing health updates and rallying around loved ones. Every ten minutes, there's a new CaringBridge site made to share updates and get support. And every hour, eighteen hundred messages of encouragement are shared on a loved one's site. CaringBridge users from around the country have shared their stories with us with the hope of helping others.

Churches have made extensive use of Facebook Groups to build community online in either open or invitation-only groups. For some churches, Facebook Groups are centered around specific hobbies, interests, or topics, ranging from sermon discussion to sports and gaming. Other churches use Facebook Groups for prayer intentions by setting up a prayer center online where people can submit their need for prayer and people can respond with prayer and support. Churches have organized groups by common interests and by location (neighborhood, city, or town). Churches conduct worship, Bible study, book groups, and more in Facebook Groups.

YouVersion, the Bible app, provides Bible Groups (www .facebook.com/YouVersion/groups) that allow people to invite one or two close friends to join you in a Bible reading plan. Each person will see one another's progress in the reading plan and they can talk over each day's reading in a private discussion area (YouVersion Bible Reading Plans: www.bible.com/reading-plans-collection/1888).

We now have the technology with online conferencing (such as Zoom, Google Meet, and Microsoft Teams) and online groups (such as Facebook Groups) to design church ministries in online formats that build community *and* promote spiritual and religious growth. Here are a variety of opportunities for building community online, designed to spark your creativity as you look for ways to connect people, build relationships, practice faith, share stories, and create community in online spaces.

Small Groups

Small groups, self-organizing or facilitated by a church leader, provide a flexible way to build communities in online spaces. Churches can provide resources, support, and training for small group leaders, thereby enabling people to organize their own small groups. Online small groups can be organized around a wide variety of topics. Here are a few examples:

- Life stage groups, such as young adults, newly married couples, new parents, older adults, and much more

- Intergenerational small groups for learning, faith sharing, prayer, service, and more

- Parent support groups, moms' groups, dads' groups

- Support groups for caregiving, recovery, grief, divorce

- Bible study groups around particular books of the Bible or a Bible reading challenge (such as reading the Bible in 365 days)

- Book reading group or video study group

- Theological study groups (book, video, or online course)

- Sunday Lectionary-based faith-sharing groups

- Weekly *lectio divina* or *visio divina* group based on the Sunday Scripture readings

- Inquiry groups and introduction to Christianity groups built around a program such as Alpha (https://alphausa .org, https://alphausa.org/catholic, and https://www .alpha.org/youth)

- New member groups

- Prayer groups

- Spiritual growth groups

- Morning or evening prayer group

- Social justice issue-oriented groups

- Social justice advocacy groups

One-to-One

Mentoring or accompaniment provides a one-to-one or one-to-a-group (family or small group) online relationship-building opportunity, such as a spiritual direction, apprenticeships, guiding people in a Christian initiation or new member process, or accompanying newly married couples or new parents. Here are a few opportunities for one-to-one or one-to-a-group mentoring:

- Spiritual direction

- Milestones (baptism, First Communion, confirmation)

- Apprenticeships

- Career and life planning

- Life transitions

- Gifts discernment

- Vocational or calling discernment and formation

- Strengths discernment

Planning a Digital Community Strategy

Gathering people virtually is not that different than gathering in person. Both require being intentional, as well as a plan, a place or platform to help execute the plan, advertising, and engaging with the people who gather. Technology is a means to an end. It is not the end itself. In the same way you would not show a video in person without a discussion afterward in a faith formation setting, you cannot do that in a virtual space. It's not that you were able to make the technology work in delivering the video that is important;

it is the conversation that helps people take what they have learned and use it on their faith journey.

Communities of faith have certain purposes in serving their members and potential members. These purposes can include teaching about the faith, praying together, supporting and/or participating in missionary work, and evangelization. In most cases, gathering together to engage in these activities is what it means to be a church. The word "community" implies the gathering together of people. Yet we can gather people virtually as well as in person. But how do we do that?

Technology and using online tools to build community can be daunting for sure. The first step in each step of the decision-making process is to pray. Prayer is always the beginning of moving forward in creating community in virtual spaces, and so a plan is necessary. It will help you lay a good foundation and framework and provide the structure needed to move forward.

Step One. Determine Purpose and Audience

1. What does your church want to accomplish?

2. Does your community truly *need* this type of virtual gathering place?

3. What aspects of discipleship am I trying to support in this community?
   - Evangelization
   - Prayer/Worship
   - Witness
   - Study
   - Service
   - Stewardship

4. Do you want to sustain existing relationships or create spaces for new ones?

5. Are you interested in starting small Christian groups within your larger faith community?

6. Who is my audience? Who will interact with people in the virtual space?
   - Ministry leaders
   - Small groups
   - Committees
   - Faith formation
   - Bible study
   - Social groups

7. Do you want to focus on a specific age demographic?

Step Two. Create a Plan

1. Find out if there are guidelines in place from your church leadership, such as media release forms or a social media policy.

2. Form an implementation team. Utilize your human resources.
   - What web tools or technology will you use?
   - What is your budget? Will your church underwrite your equipment needs?
   - Who will be responsible to learn how to use it? To implement it? To monitor it? It is always a good practice to have more than one person know the basics of using a web tool including user name, passwords, and basic functions of a program or tool.
   - How will you communicate what you are doing to the group you are targeting?
   - How will you plan advertising and a way to sign up/opt in?

- What kinds of publicity materials do you need? Consider your branding, graphics, logo, links to online resources already on your website, etc.

- How will you register people and what registration materials do you need?

3. Schedule the rollout of your plan. Include time for practice with a small group before going out to the whole group.

4. Decide on how and when you will assess the effectiveness of your plan.

Step Three. Implement the Plan

1. Set the start date.

2. Advertise and begin sign-ups.

3. Provide easy, personal, and ongoing training to participants in using the technology or web tool as needed.

4. Go live.

5. Offer support to leaders and participants when using new technology.

Step Four. Periodic Assessment

1. Assess the technology/web tool as well as people's response to it.

2. Fine-tune the plan.

3. Decide on what is next. Should you go deeper into this program or add something new?

4. Evaluate the project. How will you measure success? Increased collections? Satisfaction surveys? New ministries in the church community? Increased participation?

Conclusion

Community discipleship in virtual spaces is an essential part of the twenty-first-century church. It is, in fact, a mission field of the modern church. More people are connected to technology than have met Jesus, and we must be committed to sharing the Good News with them. More people are online than will ever walk into the doors of your church, and we must meet them where they are with the Good News. We must be willing and trained to accompany them in healthy and godly relationships online.

These goals are achievable if we approach them with an open mind and a willingness to learn. This shift will need more than just one person to make it happen. It will take people with skills in technology, communication, and design—people who are creative, not afraid of technology, and maybe a bit adventurous. We can establish and maintain the church online if we can cultivate the infrastructure to support technology and attract the human hearts to sustain the relationships that we form there.

Being a part of the digital world is not much different than Paul in his travels in the first century. Like Paul, who used letters to keep in touch with the churches he founded, we can use technology to stay in touch with our church. We can reach out to those who are lost or afraid or need to hear a good word. If we do not engage with people using technology, we risk becoming irrelevant. Without an online presence, we are not viable in the twenty-first century. With an online presence that is rich with disciples engaging in prayer, worship, evangelization, service, and the love of God, our church will have a vibrant online presence today.

CHAPTER FOUR

Faith Formation in the Digital Age

John Roberto

In an earlier era of faith formation, if you wanted to learn more about the Bible, spirituality, or theology, you could take a course at a fixed time—at a church, seminary, college, or other education provider. Or you could read a book, perhaps recommended by your pastor and borrowed from your church library, or you could watch a video—on VHS, of course! Your options would have been limited by both time and space. In the twenty-first century, if you want to learn more about the Bible, spirituality, theology, or just about any other topic or interest, your options have greatly expanded.

Today, among many options, you can engage in any combination of the following learning experiences to learn about prayer and how to pray:

- Take a course on prayer or spiritual disciplines at church or at a college or a seminary.

- Take an online course—at a scheduled time with a group or at your own time and pace—using a course like "On Prayer" by Dr. Lawrence Cunningham (https://mcgrath.nd.edu/online-courses/step/courses/on

-prayer) or "Centering Prayer" by Cynthia Bourgeault (https://www.spiritualityandpractice.com/ecourses /course/view/114/centering-prayer).

- Read a book on prayer like *Learning to Pray: A Guide for Everyone* by James Martin or form a book group to read the book together.

- Listen to audio versions of books on prayer, such as *Learning to Pray*, as you commute to work each day.

- Watch the six videos on learning how to pray by James Martin on YouTube: https://www.youtube .com/playlist?list=PLFA_2Z1L-3trG2uB4ghong _QNUTU7j1qB.

- Pray online (alone or with a group) at The Upper Room Prayer Center—an intercessory prayer ministry: http://prayer-center.upperroom.org.

- Use an app to develop the practice of prayer like Pray as You Go (https://pray-as-you-go.org), Pray.com (https://www.pray.com), or Daily Prayer (https:// www.rethinkme.com).

- Learn about the Ignatian approach to prayer—the spiritual exercises, the daily examen, and more—at Ignatian Spirituality: www.ignatianspirituality.com /ignatian-prayer.

- Join a prayer group at church or another local church.

- Find a prayer guide or spiritual director in your church or area who will guide you in developing your prayer life.

- Create a blog to post your thoughts on what you are learning and invite others to offer their insights.

- Organize your own learning group by gathering a group of people who are interested in learning more about prayer and how to pray using print, audio, video, and/or online resources to guide your small group.

This example illustrates the dramatic shift in how we learn today. We now have the ability to construct our own networks of learning, utilizing a variety of new technologies and the abundance of high-quality print, audio, video, and online resources that are readily available to us. Learning networks not only provide access to a virtually endless array of opportunities; they also offer us multiple points of entry, providing individualized pathways of learning and faith growth.

We are witnessing a transformation in the way we think about learning, reflecting the convergence of new technologies, digital media and tools, and network thinking. We are shifting *from education to learning*—digital media and technologies enable learning anywhere, anytime; *from consumption of information to participatory learning*—organized around learners' interests, enabling them to create as well as consume information; and *from institutions to networks*— where people of all ages can learn from a variety of sources in a variety of settings.

These key transformations need to be central to faith formation: putting learners at the center of our thinking, enabling and trusting them to be cocreators of their learning experiences, connecting learning authentically to life concerns and real-world issues, making room for new modes of learning and new methods of teaching, fostering collaboration, and organizing structures around learners' needs.

The digital transformation is making possible new approaches for developing faith formation programming. Consider what is possible today because of the digital transformation:

- Learning and faith formation are now mobile—anytime, anyplace, 24-7. People have the digital devices to stay connected and to access learning and faith formation on the go. We can "program" faith formation experiences around people's interests and time.

- There is an abundance of high-quality digital content for faith formation—audio, video, print, websites, apps, online learning platforms, and more.

- New digital media and learning methods provide multiple ways to learn and grow, including activities and experiences that reflect different learning styles and multiple intelligences.

- Digital media and online activities, especially videos, mean that we can develop content in smaller units (micro-learning) that better suit today's learners who have shorter attention spans.

- Websites can serve as centers of faith formation with digital playlists, online courses, and resources for families and all ages.

- Online classrooms, like Edmodo, Schoology, Seesaw, and Google Classroom provide safe spaces for people to engage in faith-forming experiences and interact.

- The abundance of content and digital methods, media, and platforms provide the tools necessary to personalize the faith formation experience for children, adolescents, adults, and families.

The Growth of Digital Approaches to Faith Formation

The digital transformation has created more options for programming. Faith formation programming can now be designed in three modes: *gathered physical settings* (churches, homes, camps, retreat centers, community places, colleges or seminaries), *online settings* (websites, social media, online communities, online classrooms, and more), and *hybrid or blended settings* that combine physical gathering with online content and experiences. One program can now be designed and delivered in three modes: gathered in person, online, and hybrid. This approach will dramatically increase the number of opportunities for faith formation for people but not increase the number of unique programs that a church creates.

Programming in gathered physical spaces has been the dominant approach to faith formation with most programs and activities offered at church, often supported by other settings such as retreat centers, service in the community, and camps. Most churches have overused gathered models as an approach to faith formation. Churches can become much more strategic and careful about when, where, how, and why we gather people "at church" because we have two additional programming approaches.

With the abundance of digital tools and media, churches can now design *online* models of faith formation by producing digital content, offering online courses and webinars, creating playlists of curated resources (courses, videos, readings, podcasts, and more), streaming live programs and presentations, providing access to online courses on a variety of topics developed by colleges and seminaries, and curating resources for the church year season and special events.

Churches can now design *hybrid* or *blended* models that integrate in-person gatherings (at church, in family groups, and small groups) *with* online faith formation experiences (such as developing playlists that provide a menu of learning experiences on the theme of the program). Hybrid models hold together two important values in faith formation: 1) the importance of in-person relationships and faith-forming experiences, and 2) the importance of being responsive to the complexity of people's lives and their religious-spiritual needs. Hybrid models expand faith formation opportunities for everyone. We can become much more intentional about when, where, how, and why we gather because we can now integrate online with in-person faith forming.

Hybridity

The concept of hybridity is not new to us. We are already living hybrid lives. Every day we weave together a life that is lived both online (mediated) and offline (in person). Faith formation is catching up to the way people already live and interact every day. Angela Gorrell, author of *Always On: Practicing Faith in a New Media Landscape*, writes about living hybrid lives:

> Recognizing online actions as meaning-filled helps Christian communities to consider our current online and in-person reality in terms of its hybridity, rather than in terms of digital dualism (think of online as virtual and in person as real). "Hybridity" describes "the coming together of online and offline, media and matter, or more dynamically . . . the interplay between the online and offline dimension." Most Americans live hybrid lives because our online and offline lives have been integrated. Interactions online shape offline experiences, and offline communication and practices shape people's online engagement.[1]

Angela Gorrell writes that we not only live hybrid lives, but we now live in hybrid Christian communities.

> Hybrid Christian communities embody God's love and "make the message believable" through meaning-

---

1. Angela Gorrell, *Always On: Practicing Faith in a New Media Landscape* (Grand Rapids, MI: Baker Academic, 2019), 47.

ful conversations and faithful habits that are both in person and mediated, that take place at various times, and that happen in both physical and digital spaces.

I do not think it is too daunting for Christian communities to think about their community as being hybrid, given Paul's letters and specifically his use of the metaphor of the "body of Christ." Paul's letters are a clear example of hybrid Christian communities, since his letters were extensions of his in-person ministry within particular communities and also provided mediated guidance for those communities.

It is possible to nurture a hybrid Christian community. Many Christian communities *are* hybrid Christian communities (though they would probably not use this terminology) because they are nurturing relationships, growing spiritually, and engaging in ministry in-person and online. Through social media, members are cultivating connections online that are not that different from the relationships that prevailed before the internet and mobile phones.[2]

The key to hybrid faith formation is the integration of in-person faith-forming with online faith-forming into *one* holistic integrated experience. A program design can begin online and then move to in person and back to online *or* it can begin in person and continue online.

Hybrid programming can be *synchronous* (real time) and *asynchronous* (on your own time)—thereby expanding the opportunities for people to engage in faith-forming experiences that are responsive to their time, commitments, and availability. We can deliver *synchronous* faith formation using physical gatherings, livestreaming, video conferencing, online courses, and online small groups. We can deliver *asynchronous* faith formation using online playlists, video

2. Gorrell, *Always On*, 50–51.

and audio programs, online discussion groups, online learning platforms, websites, and more.

A good example of the practice of hybridity is The Slate Project (https://www.slateproject.org). It is a new style of Christian community that recognizes that people gather both online and face-to-face to follow Jesus. They offer the following mix of experiences that utilize the best of in-person gathering and online experiences and interaction:

- #Breaking Bread: Offering Christian worship rooted in the ancient arts, with a home-cooked meal, unique community, and prayers (in person Mondays at 6 p.m.).

- #WakeUpWordUp: Recovering the Bible as a story worth telling (in person Tuesday at 10 a.m.).

- Engaging Images: Creating unique image-based content on Wednesday (#WednesdayWisdom) that looks to engage with a twenty-first-century Christianity.

- #SlateSpeak: Meeting on Twitter with a live-chat, weekly, topical discussion with a new moderator each week (Thursdays at 9 p.m.).

- #SlateReads: Meeting on Twitter with a live-chat book discussion group.

- Audio/Video Content: Releasing a monthly video/podcast (first Saturdays) that engages with different relevant topics in our world and our church and provides resources for our partners in ministry to use.

Digitally Integrated Approaches to Faith Formation

The following section presents a variety of ways to structure faith formation using *hybrid approaches* that blend physical and online settings, and *online approaches* that use online platforms for all programming. The examples below are offered as suggestions to help with your planning and spark your own creativity in designing faith formation using digital platforms, tools, methods, and media.

1. Hybrid Approaches

One way to develop hybrid programming is by beginning with in-person faith formation and then deepening it with online faith formation. We can extend the theme of an in-person event or program by curating a variety of faith-forming experiences that provide more depth and application of the theme through images, video, audio, and readings. We can deliver the content using a multimedia newsletter, social media posts, and/or a playlist on a website. Here are several examples you can adapt. Consider designing programs like mission trips, Vacation Bible School, and retreats in hybrid models.

Worship and Online Formation

- Participate in Sunday worship (in person or livestreamed). (Synchronous)

- Engage in faith-forming activities online using an all-ages playlist on Sunday's theme: prayers, readings, video, podcast, art, music, creative activities, conversations, and action ideas. (Asynchronous) This approach can easily be applied to a gathered event.

In-Person and Online Formation

- Meet in person once per month (or every other week). (Synchronous)

- Engage in online faith formation for the other weeks of the month using a playlist on the theme. (Asynchronous)

In-Person and Online Formation with Video Meetings

- Week 1: Meet in person for the program. (Synchronous)

- Week 2: Engage in online faith-forming experiences using a playlist on the theme. (Asynchronous)

- Week 3: Continue with the playlist learning on the theme. (Asynchronous)

- Week 4: Conduct an in-person or video meeting (Zoom) for small groups or age groups or families to discuss and apply the online learning. (Synchronous)

In-Person and Livestreamed or Video and Online

- Week 1: Meet in person for the program. (Synchronous)

- Week 2: Engage in online faith-forming experiences using a playlist on the theme. (Asynchronous)

- Week 3: Conduct a livestream presentation, demonstration, or prerecorded video (using Zoom, Facebook Live, or YouTube Live) on the theme of the month's program. (Synchronous)

- Week 4: Continue with playlist learning on the theme. (Asynchronous)

A second way to develop a hybrid model is to begin with online faith formation, leading to in-person experiences. This approach is known as flipped learning, in which direct instruction moves from the group learning space to the individual learning space online, and the group space is transformed into a dynamic interactive learning environment where the leader/teacher guides participants as they creatively discuss, practice, and apply the content.

Online and Monthly Gathering

- Create a blog post or newsletter or online playlist on the theme of the month, and give people time to engage in their own learning. (Asynchronous)

- Participate in a large group or small group gathering to discuss, reflect, and apply the theme of the month. (Synchronous)

Online and Small Group Gatherings (Asynchronous)

- Week 1: Engage in online learning using Playlist #1 on the theme. (Asynchronous)

- Week 2: Participate in a small group gathering to discuss and apply the learning (in person or through video conferencing). (Synchronous)

- Week 3: Engage in online learning using Playlist #2 on the theme. (Asynchronous)

- Week 4: Participate in a small group gathering to discuss and apply the learning in person or through video conferencing. (Synchronous)

Flipped Learning

Flipped learning is very helpful when it is difficult to gather people consistently. This approach is well suited to preparation for marriage, parent preparation for baptism, First Communion with parents and children, and confirmation. We can *prepare* people online with the appropriate content (experiences, activities, video/audio, and resources), then *engage* them in person for sessions or the event, and *sustain and apply* the experience through online faith formation.

A good example of this is an adolescent confirmation program. Here is a flipped approach illustrated in a monthly format for young people that can be woven into a yearlong program.

- *On Your Own*: Engage young people with a monthly learning playlist—watching videos, reading short articles, praying, writing reflections in a journal—on the theme. (Asynchonous)

- *In a Small Group*: Have young people participate in one small group experience (online or face-to-face) to discuss the content in the playlist and what they are learning. (Synchronous)

- *In a Large Group*: Involve young people in a monthly meeting with all groups for community sharing, interactive activities, short presentations, and ideas for living faith. (Synchronous)

2. Online-Only Approaches

Churches can develop fully online programming (asynchronous) by offering independent (on-your-own) faith formation using the abundance of online programs and resources for all ages, especially adults. Leaders can curate courses and resources from seminaries, universities, and Christian publishers and organizations. It is helpful to use a thematic approach to organize playlists or web pages with self-directed learning topics like Scripture, prayer and spiritual formation, social justice issues, theological themes, morality and ethics, and much more.

Churches can develop a complete online faith formation experience with content and experiences such as an online Advent curriculum that connects the Advent events at church with online content for experiencing Advent in daily and home life. The online experiences can include prayer activities, daily Bible readings, daily devotions, Advent study resources, videos, and service activities.

Churches can use video conferencing to create webinars, such as a monthly theology presentation for adults or a monthly one-hour parent formation. A parent webinar series can be designed around the knowledge, skills, and practices for faith-forming and effective parenting, as well as using guest presenters to conduct the webinars. A church could blend the monthly webinars with one- or two-parent dinners (childcare or parallel children's programming provided) during the year for parents to gather in person to meet each other and discuss what they are learning through webinars.

Here are two examples of programming that is primarily online with interactive features.

Online Only

- Week 1: Livestream (or video recording) of the class, program, or presentation. (Synchronous)

- Weeks 2–3: Online learning experiences using a playlist for the content/activities on a website. (Asynchronous)

- Week 4: Facebook Group (or online learning platform) for engaging people in discussion and presenting projects. (Synchronous or asynchronous)

Online with Interaction

- Week 1: Livestream of the class, program, or presentation. (Synchronous)

- Week 2: Online learning experiences using a playlist for the content/activities on a website. (Asynchronous)

- Week 3: Zoom meetings for small groups or family groupings. (Synchronous)

- Week 4: Online learning experiences using a playlist for the activities/content. (Asynchronous)

Add an interactive feature by using a Facebook Group (or online learning platform) to engage people in discussion, sharing learning, and presenting projects.

One Program, Multiple Programming Models

With multiple ways to program in physical, online, and hybrid spaces, one program or experience can be designed in all three spaces, increasing the availability to a wider audience of people. The choice is no longer whether to participate or not, but which option best suits a person's time, schedule, and learning preferences.

Imagine taking a four-session, video-based, online course on a topic in theology, Scripture, social issues, or life-stage issues and offering it in all three spaces.

1. *Large group physical gathering*: People gather at church and a leader facilitates the program—showing the video presentation, providing time for people to read and reflect, and guiding small groups in discussing the content.

2. *Small group physical gathering*: People gather in small groups in homes or coffee shops or other conducive setting, watch the video, and then read, reflect on, and discuss the content.

3. *Small group hybrid*: People gather online in a small group (Zoom or other video conferencing platform) to watch the video together, read and reflect on the content, and discuss the content.

4. *Online with interaction*: People complete the sessions on their own and share reflections in a Facebook group (asynchronous) or meet on Zoom to discuss the program (synchronous).

5. *Online independent*: People complete the learning program on their own.

The "one program, multiple models" approach can be used in designing programming for families and all ages. It dramatically increases the offerings on the faith formation network and gives control to people so they can choose what and when and how and where they will learn.

Digital Playlists for Faith Formation

The digital playlist has become an essential resource for designing hybrid and online faith formation. What the textbook was to the print era, the playlist is to the digital world. It provides the learning content in an interactive, personalized, multimedia format—with a variety of ways to learn and experience the content.

The idea of a playlist is simple: it is a sequence of activities and resources on a topic designed for individual and/or small-group learning, usually available on a digital form. Playlists make faith formation available at any time. They are a way to personalize faith formation around the needs and interests of each life stage and the diversity of people's spiritual and religious needs. Playlists make the learner of any age the center of faith formation, providing multiple ways to grow in faith. The responsibility for learning and growing in faith shifts from the provider to the person.

An education playlist is similar in concept to a music playlist, in which a person curates music from a variety of artists into a group of songs selected because they are favorites, are from the same musical genre, or are on a similar theme. Faith formation playlists are topical and can be designed for a season of the church year, a theological topic, a biblical story or teaching, a social concern, a life-cycle issue, and more.

Playlists can be designed using a *menu approach* of faith-forming activities where people select activities that address their needs, interests, or time availability. Playlists can also be designed using a *sequenced approach* using a learning process to structure the faith formation experiences and activities. Playlists can include synchronous (real-time, scheduled) activities and asynchronous (on-your-own) activities.

Playlists can be published on a website, in a learning management system (Google Classroom, Edmodo, Seesaw), or even in a newsletter or blog that allows for video to be embedded. Social media, especially Instagram, is useful for sharing learning projects and reflections. It is important that the playlists are available 24-7 on a digital platform. Creating a faith formation website (lifelong or for targeted audiences) is often the best option. Building a website is made much easier today by the availability of online website builders that provide predesigned website templates, drag-and-drop features to create web pages, and hosting for the website.

For examples of faith formation playlists, go to the Family Faith Playlists section of the Michigan Conference UMC website to view (or use) the playlists developed by Rev. Kathy Pittenger at https://michiganumc.org/playlists. For a curated list of playlists, go to my website at www .LifelongFaith.com.

Approach 1. A Menu of Faith Formation Activities

In the menu approach, activities and experiences are organized into categories. Create a menu for an individual topic or event by curating a variety of ways to explore and experience a season of the church year, a theological topic, a biblical story or teaching, a social concern, or a life-cycle issue. Here is an example of a menu approach for studying the Gospel of Luke. Each of the offerings would include a description of the activity and a link to the activity (if it is not included within the playlist).

Read

- Learn about the Gospel of Luke at Enter the Bible: outline, background, introductory issues, and theological themes at EntertheBible.org.

- Read *Luke for Everyone: Bible Study Guide* by N. T. Wright (IVP Connect).

Watch

- Explore the Gospel of Luke in a five-part, animated video series from the Bible Project at BibleProject.com.

- Watch the *Gospel of Luke* movie on Netflix. Word-for-word Bible texts of the entire book of Luke are narrated and reenacted in this epic production of Luke's accounts of Jesus' life on Netflix.

Participate

- Join an eight-session online Bible study of the Gospel of Luke on Yale Bible Study with Dr. David L. Bartlett and Dr. Allen R. Hilton at YaleBibleStudy.org.

Listen

- Listen to the audio program "How to Read and Understand the Gospel of Luke and the Acts of the Apostles," by Fr. William L. Burton, OM, SSL, STD, at Learn25 .com.

Pray and Reflect

- Participate in *A Journey with Luke: The 50 Day Bible Challenge* by Marek P. Zabriskie. Join the journey with Luke with fifty days of Scripture readings, meditations, and prayers written by dynamic spiritual leaders from around the world at ForwardMovement.org.

Here is an example of a Lent seasonal playlist for children and parents. The abundance of digital content for the seasons of the church year and for Sunday worship and the Lectionary make it easy to curate and design seasonal playlists. Each activity would be described with links to the activities (if not included on the web page).

Read

- Daily devotional for Lent for children and for adults/ parents
- Children's storybooks on the themes of each Sunday's Lectionary readings from Storypath at StoryPath .upsem.edu
- Daily Scripture readings

Watch

- Video: "Lent in 3 Minutes" introduction to Lent video from Busted Halo (https://bustedhalo.com)
- Video: "Ash Wednesday and Lent" from Chuck Knows Church video commentary for each Sunday gospel reading in Lent (https://chuckknowschurch.com)

Participate

- Sunday worship
- Friday Lenten soup suppers
- Stations of the Cross

Pray and Reflect

- Daily Lenten prayers
- Ash Wednesday service at home

Experience

- Lenten calendar with short activities for each day

- Creative arts activities for each Sunday of Lent and Holy Week

- Visual Stations of the Cross

Serve

- Make a meal for someone who is homebound.

- Collect groceries for the food pantry.

- Participate in the Church World Service CROP Walk.

Approach 2. Sequenced Learning on a Topic or Theme

In the *sequenced* approach, a learning process structures the faith formation experiences and activities on the playlist. Playlists can include synchronous (real-time, scheduled) activities and asynchronous (on-your-own) activities. An excellent process for learning, based on the 4MAT learning cycle developed by Dr. Bernice McCarthy (see https://aboutlearning.com), has four movements: experience the topic, explore knowledge about the topic, practice and demonstrate personal learning, and perform and present the learning.

Here is an example of how the four-step process can be applied to playlist design for a four-session mini-course on a theme or topic with synchronous and asynchronous activities. This example can easily be redesigned into an asynchronous playlist, especially after the live session in Week One is video recorded. It's also a way to use your curriculum resources and programming in a playlist format.

Week 1. Engage the learner in the topic or theme (synchronous)

Key design questions to address: First ask, "Why?" Why is this of value to the person? Why do they need to know this? Then ask what you will do to get people excited about the content of the session. What experience will you create that will inspire them to learn? What techniques will you use to give them an opportunity to share what they experienced?

Example: Begin the playlist with a synchronous live-streamed session (on Zoom or Facebook Live or YouTube Live) to gather the group, introduce the topic/theme, and show how it connects to the life of the learner. One or more methods can be used, such as a combination of presentation, demonstration, video, storytelling, and even participant contributions if you use Zoom. (The first week presentation could also be a face-to-face gathering.)

Week 2. Explore the topic or theme (asynchronous)

Key design questions to address: First ask, "What?" What needs to be known about this topic? Then ask how you will engage people in developing their knowledge and understanding of the topic.

Example: Learners select one or more activities that go deeper into the topic or theme. This can take many forms: video, audio, text, reading, prayer, or ritual.

Week 3. Practice and demonstrate learning (asynchronous)

Key design questions to address: First ask, "How?" How will this be of use in people's lives? This is where learners take the learning and do something with it, something that has meaning for them. This is where they demonstrate relevance.

Example: Learners use a variety of methods to create an activity, individually or with others in the group, that demonstrates learning. They can use one or more learning apps (see Resource at the end of this chapter for a list of learning apps with the best reviews) to design a creative project that demonstrates their learning.

Week 4. Perform and present the project (synchronous)

Key design questions to address: First ask, "What if?" Then ask, what will people be able to do that they can't do now? How will learners explain or perform their work? The word "per-form" means to form through, and that is the essence of this step. It represents the merging of the learning and the learner.

Example: The conclusion of the mini-course engages the learners in presenting their projects to demonstrate their learning. This can be a done in a face-to-face setting or online using Zoom or other video conferencing tools.

Twenty-First-Century Learning Methods for Faith Formation

We know that people of all ages, especially younger generations, learn best in environments that are safe, welcoming, interactive, participatory, experiential, visual, and multisensory. We can dramatically improve our effectiveness in promoting growth and learning in faith by using these new approaches. They are enhanced using digital technologies, methods, and media. Here are brief descriptions of methods that can be used in designing faith formation programs and experiences. Some of these approaches and methods may be best suited for younger generations, but in some form, most of these can be utilized across the life cycle.

Personalized Learning is tailoring the learning environment—what, when, how, and where people learn—to address the individual needs, skills, and interests of each person. Personalization asks, "What is best for you?" Personalization engages learners in creating personal learner plans—customized learning paths—for people to work at their own pace, alone or with a group.

Micro-Learning experiences are short-form (five, ten, and fifteen minutes) learning experiences designed for anywhere, anytime learning that be combined into multipart learning programs. Micro-learning experiences are one response to short attention spans and mobile learning. We can create and curate micro-learning experiences on a topic using play-lists to engage people in all types of faith formation content. Breaking content into small learning units enhances comprehension and retention of knowledge, skills, and practices.

Project-Based Learning is a method in which learners gain knowledge and skills by working for an extended period of time to investigate and respond to an authentic, engaging, and complex question, problem, or challenge. Learners are actively engaged in real-world and personally meaningful projects. They demonstrate their knowledge and skills by creating a public product or presentation for a real audience. As a result, they develop deep content knowledge as well as critical thinking, collaboration, creativity, and communication skills.

Collaborative Learning involves small, noncompetitive groups where learners can discuss and process together what they are learning, work together on projects and activities, and practice and present what they are learning. Learning spaces are organized for learners' participation in a "learning community"—recognizing that learning takes place in a social context and relies on communication and interaction with others. All ages, especially the younger generations, learn best in an environment where they can share with and cocreate their education with their peers. Collaborative learning requires creating an environment that is safe, caring, accepting, and trustworthy so that people feel free to share, discuss, and question.

Multiple Intelligences Learning brings the eight multiple intelligences into learning experiences, providing a greater variety of ways for people to learn: verbal-linguistic (word smart, book smart), logical-mathematical (number smart, logic smart), visual-spatial (art smart, picture smart), bodily-kinesthetic (body smart, movement smart), musical-rhythmic (music smart, sound smart), naturalist (nature smart, environment smart), interpersonal (people smart, group smart), and intrapersonal (self-smart, introspection smart). While not every program can incorporate activities for all eight intelligences, a greater variety of ways to learn promotes more effective learning and engages people more fully in the learning experience.

Multisensory Learning utilizes all the senses in a learning experience where people can taste, smell, touch, and hear things related to the topic of the session. Multisensory learning sees the world as a canvas to paint with words, sights, sounds, video, music, web pages, and more. Multimedia means using multiple modalities to engage people in the learning experience.

Visual Learning guides people in learning to "read" or interpret visual images and how to use visual images to communicate. Visual literacy includes interpreting, understanding, and appreciating the meaning of visual images, communicating more effectively by applying the basic principles and concepts of visual design, and producing visual images in digital formats.

Practice-Oriented Learning means incorporating real-life-application activities into the learning experience. Practice is a part of the learning process, not the result of it. Research is demonstrating that people learn more deeply when they apply knowledge to real-world problems and when they take part in projects that require sustained engagement and collaboration. Learning programs provide opportunities to apply new knowledge and skills by practicing in as realistic a setting as possible. Activities that involve thoughtful responses, decision-making, and solving problems encourage active learning and promote higher-order thinking.

Storytelling enlivens learning by creating and telling stories, presenting case studies, and showing examples. Digital storytelling provides new ways to engage in storytelling through images, audio, video, and in digital spaces such as Instagram.

Immersive Learning Experiences are highly relational, interactive, participatory, experiential, visual, and multisensory. Churches already offer these types of experiences (Vacation Bible School, retreats, mission trips), often as special programs. Churches can expand immersive faith-forming opportunities to include a variety of extended-time programs (half day, full day, weekend, weeklong) offered throughout the year on a variety of topics. Imagine the level of engagement and interest if all children's programming was like Vacation Bible School or youth programming like a mission trip or retreat experience.

Conclusion

Hybrid and online-only models will continue to become more and more central to all faith formation programming. Hybrid models hold together two important values in faith formation: the importance of in-person relationships and faith-forming experiences, and the importance of being responsive to the complexity of people's lives and their religious-spiritual needs by using digital tools. Hybrid and online-only models expand faith formation opportunities for everyone. We can become much more strategic and careful about when, where, how, and why we gather people because we can now integrate online with in-person faith-forming. We will continue to find that hybrid models of faith formation are more resilient, flexible, inclusive, and adaptable—just what we need to respond to the challenges of change in our world and in lives of our people!

Resource. A Guide to Digital Learning Methods Apps

The following digital tools have been selected because of their ability to be used in learning and faith formation. They include websites and apps, and often both formats. Most are free or have a low-cost subscription. The American Association of School Librarians does a yearly review of the best websites, tools, and resources for teaching and learning. Check out the ALA website at www.ala.org/aasl /standards-guidelines/best-websites and www.ala.org /aasl/awards/best.

Anchor: For creating high-quality podcasts with free and easy-to-use creation tools and hosting service that includes a variety of sound effects and audio clips (https://anchor.fm).

Animoto: For creating videos from your photos, video clips, music, and text (http://animoto.com and https://animoto .com/business/education).

Book Creator: For engaging in the real-world application of online publishing by creating and publishing fiction, nonfiction, comic books, picture books, how-to guides, and more (https://bookcreator.com/).

Brush Ninja: For making animated GIFs (elementary and up) (https://brush.ninja).

Chatterpix Kids: For giving photos a voice by taking a picture, drawing a line to make a mouth, and recording your voice (http://www.duckduckmoose.com/educational-iphone -itouch-apps-for-kids/chatterpix).

Clips: For turning your iPhone into a video production studio by creating and editing dynamic videos with the ability to add subtitles, animated stickers, filters, and music, all within the app (https://www.apple.com/clips).

Deck.Toys: For creating interactive lessons with paths and activities for students to follow (https://deck.toys).

Edpuzzle: For making any video your lesson by finding a video, adding questions, and assigning it to the group—a great resource for the flipped classroom (https://edpuzzle.com).

Edublogs: For creating multimedia blogs that include videos, photos, and podcasts—all in a safe, easy, and secure environment (https://edublogs.org).

Flipgrid: For engaging and empowering every voice in a class or at home by recording and sharing short, awesome videos (https://info.flipgrid.com).

Genially: For creating presentations, infographics, video presentations, resumés, and more with templates with access to photos, animations, and illustrations, giving the user the ability to make any image or text interactive (grades: 6–8) (https://www.genial.ly).

Glogster: For creating online multimedia posters that combine images, graphics, audio, video, and text on one digital canvas (http://edu.glogster.com).

GooseChase: For creating and facilitating scavenger hunts with mobile technology to create exciting learning (elementary+) (https://www.goosechase.com).

Green Screen by Do Ink: For making it easy to animate, draw, and create incredible green-screen videos and photos by combining images from multiple sources into a single video (http://www.doink.com).

LiveBinders: For creating online binders with digital content: websites, audio, video, and text (http://www.livebinders.com/welcome/education).

Kapwing: For creating everything from video montages and memes to stop-action videos and sound effects (grades 4 and up) (https://www.kapwing.com).

Loom: For creating screencast and webcam video presentations, how-to videos, and more (grades 4 and up) (https://www.loom.com).

Magisto: For creating polished short videos from photos and video clips using a smart video editor to create a video story (https://www.magisto.com).

Nearpod: For creating interactive lessons in a 1:1 setting by easily importing existing lessons (PDFs, JPEGs, PowerPoints) and adding interactive features such as virtual field trips, 3D objects, quizzes, polls, open-ended questions, etc. (https://nearpod.com).

NowComment: For having rich, engaging discussions in both large and small groups that allow people to converse about documents, videos, and images (grades 5 and up) (https://nowcomment.com).

Padlet: For creating beautiful boards, documents, and web pages that are easy to read and fun to contribute to (https://padlet.com).

PhotoPeach: For creating digital storytelling using photos, music, and more in a slideshow (https://photopeach.com).

Pixie: For creating digital stories, nonfiction pages, comics, or podcasts with little instruction to share ideas, imagination, and understanding through a combination of text, original artwork, voice narration, and images (https://www.tech4learning.com/pixie).

PowToon: For creating animated videos and presentations, including converting a PowerPoint presentation into a video

(https://www.powtoon.com and https://www.powtoon
.com/edu-home).

PuppetMaster: For creating animation that can bring to life
any image, just by acting things out in front of the cam-
era with recorded voice, resulting in an animated video
(preschool–middle school) (https://www.shmonster.com
/puppetmaster).

Quizlet: For creating digital flashcards and generating interactive games (https://quizlet.com).

Stop Motion Studio: For creating stop-action movies with a
frame-by-frame editor, backgrounds, foregrounds, sound effects, paintbrushes, and more (https://www.cateater.com).

Tour Creator: For building immersive, 360-degree tours right
from a computer with photos, points of interest, image over-
lays, boxes with informational text, and "Did you know?"
points of interest (https://arvr.google.com/tourcreator).

Typito: For creating videos incorporating icons, shapes,
photos, and audio and video files (grades 4 and up) (https://
typito.com/social).

Wakelet: For creating playlists and newsletters by curating and creating stories with links, images, notes, titles,
PDFs, YouTube and Vimeo videos, Tweets, Facebook and
Instagram posts, Google or Dropbox documents, Sound-
cloud tracks, Spotify playlists, Google Maps, and Flipgrid
responses (https://wakelet.com).

WeVideo: For video creation, with a media library of stock
videos, images, and music tracks (https://www.wevideo
.com).

CHAPTER FIVE

Curation of Digital Media for Ministry and Faith Formation

Marge Babcock

The digital age provides access to whatever information one needs. Searching for this information can lead to more information than one is seeking, as interesting information attracts us and draws us off our original search.

I wonder if you have ever had the experience of searching for a topic, only to be pulled off course into other websites and blog pages. All the while, your mind is creating possibilities of using the new information that you weren't looking for when you started the search. In pursuing the search, our eyes have viewed pages of content that interest and attract us. Suddenly, time passes, and we need to refocus in order to complete the task at hand.

Enter the world of curation. The restrictions of the amount of time and the need to find appropriate information efficiently drive the need to find ways to organize and strategize the ways we approach looking for information and content digitally. Content that meets the needs of those who see our digital platforms needs to be pertinent and relevant. People are capable of finding information on the Web, but curated content that connects to the needs of those we serve keeps them coming back to our sites and can ultimately build positive relationships.

Part One. The Skills of Curation

So why do church leaders need to find people with the gifts and skills of a curator? A curator is someone who possesses the skills and uses digital tools of curation. Whether this is managed by an individual or as a team approach, a leader needs to be able to identify and designate who and how digital curation will be accomplished. This chapter addresses the role of the curator by outlining the following skills:

1. A curator understands the audience and their needs for using the resources.

2. A curator approaches the task of finding resources with persistence and constancy.

3. A curator builds a database of authoritative sources to consult for future curation.

4. A curator knows the mission statement, values, and objectives of the organization to inform the evaluation of content.

5. A curator maintains published content by reviewing systematically.

6. A curator uses digital tools and strategies to save resources.

1. A curator understands the audience and their needs for using resources.

In church settings it might sound like a luxury to have someone designated to do curating. Yet so much content on a website depends on good curating. The curator needs to be someone who works closely with the ministry team. Having a good sense of what people who are using the website are seeking is the first organizing task when deciding what websites, blogs, or video/audio content on which to focus one's attention.

This can be accomplished by finding ways to communicate directly with the website users in a variety of ways. If the group gathers for meetings or conferences, it might be an opportunity during breaks to ask specific people what they are working on in their ministry. What would help them with their projects and programming? Engaging in these types of conversations helps the curator know that their work is useful, as well as letting the audience know that someone is interested in supporting their work.

Using the comments on a blog page on the website is another way to communicate with website users. Some content that engages readers can be created by the curator and ministry team, and by opening the content to comments, it lets the reader audience know that there is interest in feedback about what content is offered on the website.

Another way to engage the reader audience is using social media like Facebook, Instagram, or Twitter occasionally. By giving examples of content that is curated on the website, there is the opportunity to attract more readers and followers of the website. A good digital tool that can help design posts for all sorts of media is Canva.com. There are free images, and one is able to choose the layout for specific social media posts.

2. A curator approaches finding content with persistence and constancy.

Digital content is necessary in order to maintain a digital presence. A work group or ministry team will need to make decisions about how and by whom this content will be either created or curated. Beginning to curate content lets you know what is already in the digital world and who is saying it. Content needs to be kept pertinent and relevant. Keeping abreast of curated content lets others know you are staying current and knowledgeable in your field of interest. It also helps you know where you need to create content that might be lacking, thus making better use of the group's precious time.

People who are contributing to the digital platforms need to find ways to establish procedures for how created and curated content will be followed. This can be organized in a number of ways, either by using content curation tools that bring the content to you or by checking in with trusted sources. However this is accomplished, it becomes an intentional task of an individual or a group of people's regular responsibilities. Whether setting aside some time each day or week, it's the regularity of the activity that will enable a knowledgeable curator to spot new content or trends.

What does a leader look for when finding the people to do curating? A good characteristic is someone who likes to learn. Always seeking new information requires reading material and knowing how it compares and contrasts to material that has already been published. A curator also needs to be disciplined and organized in order to keep a routine schedule of seeking information.

3. A curator builds a database of authoritative sources to consult for future curation.
In knowing the mission and vision of the church organization, a curator can find sources, digital content on the Web, that can be referred to when beginning the curation of a new topic. Credible sources are important so that the information is reliable and appropriate. When first evaluating a source, the curator must take a thorough look at the entire website or blog to identify the group, authors, and perspective being offered. It is important to pay attention to the "About" menu option, and the bottom of the web page will often give the author's biographical information. If a person is unfamiliar or unknown, an online search may be done to find any other biographical information and additional posts that the author may have done.

Credible sources come from sites that can be trusted to have authoritative information. The material has been researched and presented in such a way that the reader is not confused by any leading positions of the author. A website or blog will be transparent about how the authors have credibility that is free from bias. A curator should be able to make decisions and judgments by assessing all aspects of credible source analysis.

Another way to approach investigation of a source is to look at other posts written on the digital platform. This gives a sense of the perspective and purpose of what is being posted. Is this perspective a fit for your purpose, or does it take readers off track?

As the church leader, communicating your own boundaries and expectations to the curator is good practice. For example, are you comfortable using other denominations' posts and on what topics? Are there authors that you feel do not speak in your organization's voice? Are there topics that you do not want to be addressed in the content?

A curator becomes more knowledgeable and familiar with credible sources while becoming familiar with published content. Looking at analytics of the platform reveals which posts are getting the most traffic. From here, decisions can be made as to the types of material for which readers are searching. Building a source list makes searching for content more efficient. A knowledgeable curator is of great value to an organization.

4. A curator knows the mission statement, values, and objectives of the church organization to inform their evaluation of content.

The digital presence of your organization needs to be the face of the work that you are trying to accomplish. Having someone who understands your mission is valuable in speaking in your authentic voice. Therefore, it is preferred that the curator is someone who works on your team or very closely with the leader.

As a curator is on the Web finding content, knowing values and the mission of the church organization will be important so that posted content will exemplify your unique identity. Churches need to be cognizant of the persons who are doing the curating, as well as those who are creating content. Seeking individuals who are trained disciples gives a leader assurance that content is coming from sources that support the church's mission. Taking any volunteer who happens to have time on their hands or likes cruising the Web is probably not the best way to get the curating done. Sometimes engaging others to look for content can be a way of training others to do the work, but then it needs to be previewed by knowledgeable and experienced curators before it is placed on the digital platform.

When a curator looks at content, one question to ask is, "Is there anything about this information that would prevent me from sharing this?" The more invested the curator is in the mission and objectives of the church, the better one will be able to spot deficiencies in the content.

What every leader will want to be aware of is that curating content in a responsible way is vital to how people outside the organization get to know your mission. It is incumbent upon the leader to keep in regular communication with the curator so that the vision of the mission is in synchronicity with the digital content. The best way to accomplish this is to have a person curating who sees their role as a calling and mission. As a disciple, this person would have a solid Christian formation in theology and Scripture.

5. A curator maintains published content by reviewing systematically.
The published content needs to be kept current, which is especially true on a website. The easiest way to do this with

regularity is by scheduling review of content as a task of curation. This is not as important on a blog or social media platform. A blog is designed to organize posts by date and categories. Social media is designed for up-to-date posting.

The working objectives of your church organization become the context for keeping content current. Sometimes posts need to be shifted around on a web page in order to keep the page looking fresh and timely. Some items may need to be archived and presented at a different time.

As a leader, it is necessary to communicate and establish priorities for what and when content is being published. If the organization is working as a team, then it is important that input be given to the curator on a timely basis. Being able to look ahead gives the curator time to find curated or created content that meets the team's current needs and topic areas.

Qualities the leader would be seeking when finding a curator are organization and consistency. The tasks of maintenance and review require a curator to keep schedules and records.

6. A curator uses digital tools and strategies to save resources.

Curators use very individual approaches when gathering resources in curating. Some use simple methods of listing things on a Google document with live links. Others use digital curation tools that are made for that purpose. While most curators rely on their list of tried-and-true websites to research, there is also the constant need to go beyond this search to discover new voices, tools, and perspectives.

In order to save time and to make curating an ongoing activity, a curator can find ways to save web links that seem of interest and then return to them later to read and discern the links worth being used for posting at a later time.

Part Two. Developing a Curation Plan

Now that we have surveyed the skills of a curator, how does one do it? Here is an outline of how to proceed:

Step 1: Become knowledgeable of people in the ministry network and online.

Begin by getting to know the people in the ministry network who have content that is needed. Some of these people will be people where a conversation can be had, and other people will be known by the content on their website. This will enable the curator to build confidence in the sources that are being used. Begin following people on blogs and social media to become acquainted with their work.

Step 2: Find ways to save the online material using digital data collection apps.

While curating on the Web, it makes things more efficient if data collection apps are used. These digital tools allow for quick cataloging while searching for resources. All offer different but similar ways to save web links. Here are some ideas of ones to use:

- *Pinterest* (www.pinterest.com) is good searching by topic/category tool, but it also has the function to set up boards which can be labeled, and "pins" can be linked to the boards.

- *Pocket* (https://getpocket.com) puts items in "pockets" (topics) by using an extension on the laptop or an app on a device to save so that you can return to them later.

- *Symbaloo* (www.symbaloo.com) saves web links on your home page in "tiles" or creates web mixes for topics/categories.

- *Livebinders* (www.livebinders.com) puts files into a binder format. Create "binders" to store web links.

Step 3: Establish categories and topics so that resources can be organized and found when needed.

Study and decide how the information you curate is going to be saved. The system used has to make sense to anyone who is going to be curating. For example, do things need to be saved by topic? What does that topic mean to you? Or are things going to be saved by age groups? Or both? Establishing how curating will be organized early will save time when one is ready to find items for posting.

Step 4: Develop a resource checklist to collect resources.

Whether a curator is working on posting to a web page or on programming, it is helpful to have a list that has been created for future curating. Here are some ideas of where to search when creating this list.

- People: teachers, youth ministers, adult formation leaders, clergy and other church leaders, faith formation leaders, blog writers, website creators, respected national presenters

- Resource center websites that have religious education as their focus from churches, colleges, seminaries, educational organizations

- Faith formation bloggers, digital tools creators, other curators

- Spirituality centers, retreat centers, monasteries, convents

- Organizational websites that relate to your ministry

- Religion publisher websites

Here are the types of resources to curate:

- Apps

- Blogs

- Videos

- Online courses

- Audio podcasts

- E-books

- Video learning programs

- Online crafts and activities

- Museum websites

- Archived programming being shared from colleagues

- Movies and music (must be purchased, as they are copyrighted)

Step 5: Establish a schedule for how often curating will be done.

Curating resources is ongoing work as new information is always being produced. As programming and posting continue, it is a good discipline to have curating as part of the work hours. Make a realistic schedule with number of hours curating, number of days per week, and/or time of day. Staying on top of favorite websites and blogs helps you keep up with current information and trends.

Step 6: Curate using the skills discussed in this chapter.

Be sure to use the skills for curation described in Part One as you create your plan:

1. Understand your audience and their needs for using resources.

2. Approach the task of finding resources with persistence and constancy.

3. Build a database of authoritative sources to consult for future curation.

4. Know the mission statement, values, and objectives of your organization.

5. Maintain published content by reviewing systematically.

6. Use digital tools and strategies to save resources.

A Story of Curation

What is it like to create a website dedicated to curating faith formation? The team from *The Strong Catholic Family Faith* website (www.catholicfamilyfaith.org) has been providing resources to support family faith since 2012. The purpose of their website is to assist Catholic parish and school leaders in finding the best and most relevant content and experiences for developing faith-filled Catholic families. The website is curated by a team of four people who have a passion for ministering and supporting Catholic family faith. As curators, each person on the team brings their experience and expertise to provide resources to parents and families.

Jim Kenma, Diane Kledzik, and Wendy Schubart shared a deep desire to serve the church by providing a digital resource to churches for strengthening family faith initiatives. This desire and their connection to the "Strong Catholic Families, Strong Catholic Youth" initiative from the National Federation for Catholic Youth Ministry became the impetus to provide parish and school leaders with high-quality resources to build strong Catholic families. In 2014, Denise Utter joined the team. When asked of the benefits in working as a team, Denise said, "working collaboratively has helped us become friends." Through common interest, common bonds are created, with the result of lasting relationships. And because these individuals are located around the country, they gain different perspectives of what is occurring in different church environments.

The team approach works best for this group of curators. They curate from their own interest and expertise and agree on scheduled deadlines for posting. Their website is focused on a range of topics that serve their readers, parents, and church ministers with an eye to keeping the website current and dynamic. For church leaders, creating digital platforms and approaches like this one allows them to "reach people in the world and not expect them to come to the source."

They say that when they were first getting started, they really embarked on new territory. They kept learning new skills and ways to think about how to curate for the needs of families.

Having several years of experience now, they have been able to hone their ability to respond to the needs of the current family situation. As a team, they discussed how to approach difficult subjects like COVID-19 response and racism. The team had in-depth discussions to address how they would approach sensitive topics and how they see the resources they provide being used. Wendy says that this prompted them to add a "caveat" to the website so that the reader would understand their purpose and how to use their own judgment when sharing resources within their family.

Another way they have reached out to families over the years was by the addition of a blog page on their site. Jim, having just begun caregiving for his grandchild, created a diary of sorts for grandparenting. This is a good example of how a website can be a combination of curated and creative posts.

The team realized that they were reaching their readers of families when they were given the New Wineskins Award for innovative approaches in faith formation by the National Conference for Catechetical Leaders.

Here are several examples of other websites dedicated to curating resources for churches:

- Building Faith: https://buildfaith.org

- Congregational Resource Guide: https://thecrg.org

- Faith Formation Ministries: https://www.crcna.org /FaithFormation.

- Lifelong Faith Studio: https://www.lifelongfaithstudio .com

CHAPTER SIX

Leadership for Digital Ministry

William Miller and John Roberto

What are the competencies—knowledge, skills, and attitudes—that pastors, ministry leaders, and faith formation leaders need in today's church communities? Two sets of competencies are essential. The first set describes the emerging twenty-first-century leadership competencies for digitally integrated ministry and faith formation in churches. The second set describes the enduring, foundational competencies that form the basis for effective pastoral leadership in every age and era.

Part 1. The New Digital Ministry Qualities and Competencies for Leadership in Today's Church

Qualities

Elizabeth Drescher and Keith Anderson describe six qualities of successful digital ministers that have emerged from their research and experience. How does your digital presence and ministry reflect these qualities? How can you enhance these qualities in your ministry?

Generous: These leaders are generous with their time, advice, and ideas. They are receptive when people reach out to them online or in person. They listen, encourage, and share their best ideas.

Humble: They don't think too highly of themselves and recognize there is always more to learn because the technologies are always changing. They understand that they are one node in a massive network, but they know that even a single node can make a difference.

Curious: They know what they don't know and are continually learning about these new and evolving technologies. They are curious about other people—not just in their congregations but in their extended community. They acknowledge, affirm, and go beyond the surface.

Willing to Experiment: They are willing to try new things and see how they go. These leaders make things, launch them, and learn from them.

Collaborative: They are great collaborators, whether they are involved in digitally facilitated or local projects. They convene people, often from across different disciplines and faith traditions, and are open to ideas that aren't their own. They don't care who gets the credit.

Kind: Perhaps the most important quality is kindness. There are far too many people online—people of faith not least among them—who traffic in negativity, cynicism, and even hate, who troll others, or who seek their self-aggrandizement. The internet and our world need a different witness. To quote a Presbyterian minister who leveraged the broadcast media of television for the sake of the Gospel, Fred Rogers: "There are three ways to ultimate success. The first way is to be kind. The second ways is to be kind. The third is to be kind."[1]

---

1. Keith Anderson and Elizabeth Drescher, *Click2Save Reboot: The Digital Ministry Bible* (New York: Church Publishing, 2018), 48.

As digital ministers, we should be compassionate, engaging, inspiring, accessible, and informative. Our witness must be real—revealing our authentic selves. "The cultivation of a consistently meaningful presence and a distinct voice helps to distinguish us, invite new relationships, and nurture existing ones among the cacophony of conversations and deluge of content in social media communities."[2] Drescher and Anderson describe seven ways that leaders develop a digital presence. Which of these roles best describe your digital presence and ministry? How can you enhance these roles in your ministry?

Activist: Provides content on social justice issues, shares their own activity, and asks people to take action.

Affirming: Is more active on other people's pages than their own, offering likes and comments.

Educational: Shares educational content on topics of interest to themselves and others.

Informational: Provides links to local or national news and other content in areas of particular interest.

Pastoral: Offers prayers and blessings, expressions of concern and support for members of a more defined (congregational, denominational, organizational) ministry community.

Social: Enjoys interacting with many people across platforms, connects social media users to one another, and shares personal context that helps to deepen connections.

Spiritual: Shares prayers, spiritual quotes, inspirational images, and music, and prays for the needs of individuals and the world.[3]

---

2. Anderson and Drescher, *Click2Save*, 37.
3. Anderson and Drescher, 58.

Competencies

Working with a team from the Digital Disciples Network and its partner organizations, Caroline Cerveny, SSJ, TOSF, then president of the network, developed a set of six competencies to guide leaders in developing their knowledge and skills for digitally integrated ministry and faith formation. These six areas included community discipleship, digital citizenship, digital communication, evangelism and faith formation, digital collaboration, and digital curation. In 2019, the Technology in Faith Formation Committee of the Archdiocese of Milwaukee built on this original work (https://www.archmil.org/ArchMil/offices/Catechesis/Technology-Competencies-for-PCL-2019.pdf).

Drawing on these two documents, the thirty-three competencies present essential knowledge and skills for digital ministry today. It's best to view each competency statement on a continuum from basic to intermediate to advanced. Identify your strengths and areas for growth for each statement. It's important to remember that no one leader needs to possess all of these competencies. It may be better to think about the competencies from a team or group perspective. Engage your team or leadership group in identifying their strengths and areas they might be interested in developing.

Leadership

1. Ability to recruit, train, and strengthen volunteers to establish a creative, contemporary, and compelling digital ministry.

2. Ability to coordinate team(s) of volunteer leaders involved in digital ministry.

Developing Relationships and Community in Digital Spaces

3. Ability to select and utilize the appropriate social media (Facebook, Instagram, Twitter, TikTok, etc.) to

connect with people, build relationships, and form faith.

4. Ability to publish or present a digital story in print, image, and video using an app, social media, and/ or website.

5. Ability to organize groups of people online using social media platforms to build relationships, share life and faith experiences, pray for people, celebrate special milestones and occasions, share inspirational insights to encourage people toward living with Christlike characteristics in their everyday lives, and more.

Acting Responsibly in the Digital World

6. Ability to act in ways that are safe, legal, and ethical in online communities and spaces.

7. Ability to cultivate and manage their digital identity and reputation in the digital world, managing personal data to maintain digital privacy and security.

8. Ability to engage in positive, safe, legal, and ethical behaviors when using digital technology, including social interactions online.

9. Ability to demonstrate an understanding of and respect for the rights and obligations of using and sharing intellectual property.

10. Ability to equip people of all ages to utilize social media and online communication in ethical ways, respecting the dignity and rights of all people.

Communicating Using Digital Technology in Online and Physical Settings

11. Ability to utilize texting and email to communicate and share spiritual and religious content with diverse audiences.

12. Ability to create a blog to share spiritual and religious content, as well as to curate blogs for particular audiences.

13. Ability to create digital forms and online surveys to determine needs, register people for programming, evaluate ministries and programs, conduct gifts and talent campaigns, and more.

14. Ability to create and present interactive messages to bring the word of God to diverse communities using digital technologies.

Using Digital Tools in Ministry and Faith Formation

15. Ability to publish or present a digital story using an app, social media, or website.

16. Ability to create a website for a ministry or for faith formation.

17. Ability to create and edit short videos for church life and faith formation, as well as to publish them in digital spaces.

18. Ability to create still and motion graphics and utilize them in digital spaces.

19. Ability to develop and monitor video channels such as YouTube and Vimeo.

20. Ability to develop livestreaming for classes, courses, and presentations, as well as to archive videos for use online.

21. Ability to convene a live meeting using interactive digital meeting platforms.

22. Ability to convene and facilitate online meetings using interactive digital meeting platforms (Zoom, Google Meet, Microsoft Team, or other platforms).

Curating Digital Content

23. Ability to research and organize digital media and resources from trusted sources such as blogs, curated Christian websites, denominational websites, and Christian organizations.

24. Ability to evaluate digital media and resources using Christian values and ethical principles.

25. Ability to connect the best and most relevant resources to programming in gathered, online, and hybrid models of ministry and faith formation.

Evangelizing and Forming Faith using Digital Platforms, Methods, Media, and Apps

26. Ability to develop new and innovative programming using digital platforms, tools, methods, and media.

27. Ability to integrate digital methods and media in faith formation programming for all ages in both physical and online settings.

28. Ability to customize and personalize faith formation activities around the religious needs and learning styles of people, using digital playlists, websites, and learning apps.

29. Ability to develop faith formation in hybrid models that integrate learning in online and physical settings.

30. Ability to develop digital playlists of multimedia faith formation content that is interactive and personalized, as well as containing a variety of ways to learn and experience the content.

31. Ability to organize and facilitate online learning using Zoom, Google Meet, Microsoft Teams, or other platforms.

32. Ability to design and use online "classrooms" for faith formation, such as Edmodo, Schoology, Seesaw, and Google Classroom.

33. Ability to design a program that uses digital methods, websites, and apps for the study of the Bible and theological topics.

Reflection on the Digital Leadership Competencies

- Which of these competencies do you consider your greatest strengths?

- Which of these competencies do you want to improve or enhance?

- Who can you identify on your team or in your community to address the competencies you will not be able to master personally?

- How can you develop a personal learning plan to strengthen the areas you identified for growth?

Part 2. The Continuing Qualities and Competencies of Leadership in Today's Church

In this fast-paced world where we are bombarded constantly with words and images, asked to make quick decisions, and implored to take action, we must have a strong foundation in the spirituality of leadership.

Leadership expert Warren Bennis observed that people do not set out to be leaders. People set out to live their lives, expressing themselves fully. When that expression is of value to others, they become leaders. "So the point is not to become a leader. The point is to become yourself, to use yourself completely—all your skills, gifts, and energies—in order to make your vision manifest. You must withhold nothing. You must, in sum, become the person that you started out to be, and enjoy the process of becoming."[4]

The following eleven qualities of Christian leadership are developed from the work of Robert Greenleaf, author of the book *Servant Leadership* and numerous books and articles on servant leadership. Greenleaf was a corporate executive turned university professor and presenter who pioneered the servant leadership approach in the business and nonprofit worlds.

These eleven qualities proposed for Christian leadership in the twenty-first century can guide you in reflecting on your own leadership style and approach—affirming your strengths and identifying areas you want to enhance or strengthen in your practice of pastoral leadership.

1. A Christian leader embraces the belief that each member of a team has unique gifts and talents.

Each member of your team has something unique to contribute to the mission. One of the leader's responsibilities is to help each one discover and utilize those gifts and talents. In some cases, they are obvious; in other cases, the diamond may still be "in the rough" and need a great deal of polishing. Take time to get to know those whom you lead, their interests, their backgrounds, their likes and dislikes. At the same time, allow them to get to know you. The time you spend with them in building a relationship of confidence and trust will pay dividends as you share, learn, and grow in your ministry together.

One of the greatest gifts that God gives us is the privilege of being cocreators, as we are invited to use our gifts and talents to build the reign of God here on earth. One of the greatest joys for any Christian leader is helping others

4. Warren Bennis, *On Becoming a Leader*, 4th ed. (New York: Basic Books, 2009), 111–12.

to learn, grow, and participate in utilizing their gifts and talents. Every project you and your team undertake benefits from the ways that you support your team by affirming their giftedness and empowering them to use their talents.

2. A Christian leader is a servant who inspires others to serve.

This is exactly the picture of leadership that Christ gave to us as he washed the feet of the disciples at the Last Supper. This example fits nicely with Greenleaf's assertion that "servant leaders are healers in the sense of making whole by helping others to a larger and nobler vision and purpose than they would likely attain for themselves."[5] Note his use of the word "inspires." This implies that the leader demonstrates passion for the cause at hand—a palpable energy—that he or she communicates in a positive and energizing fashion.

Greenleaf highlights the importance of this principle when he writes "it is terribly important that one know, both about oneself and about others, whether the net effect of one's influence on others enriches, is neutral, or diminishes and depletes."[6] He cites the example of Pope John XXIII, who had a profound impact on Greenleaf's vision of effective leadership. Under the leadership of John XXIII, "for a brief moment in history (four short years) many literate persons in the Western world felt a lift of spirit, they became more significant as persons, they gathered strength to contend with the forces that were grinding them down."[7] Bringing a positive, inspiring attitude to all you do with your team will help create an environment where all mem-

5. Robert Greenleaf, *Servant Leadership: A Journey into the Nature of Legitimate Power and Greatness*, 25th ed. (Mahwah, NJ: Paulist Press, 2002), 240.

6. Greenleaf, *Servant Leadership*, 56.

7. Greenleaf, 247.

bers want to be there and feel free to be creative, bringing their own "best selves" to the work at hand.

3. A Christian leader is responsible for identifying, developing, and nurturing future leaders.

An effective leader empowers others to develop their gifts and talents. A leader concentrates on being a mentor to those on the team who are interested in learning more about their craft. Greenleaf sees this as a very important responsibility; building a team whose members "grow taller and become healthier, stronger, more autonomous."[8] Few tasks are more worthwhile or more satisfying than helping another person realize their leadership potential while growing in their relationship with God and with the faith community they serve.

4. A Christian leader models justice.

Pastoral leaders lead from a clear set of core values and personal principles. In the words of Chris Lowney about Pope Francis: "great leadership is 'incarnational'—that is, leaders imitate Jesus, who willingly plunged into a messy world and nonetheless remained undeterred from his vision of how human beings ought to treat one another."[9] Greenleaf, a self-proclaimed optimist by nature, describes the servant leader as one who accepts the limitations imposed by injustice as a foundation upon which the leader can build toward wholeness through adventurous and creative achievement.

As Christian leaders, we must constantly ask ourselves: How do our actions, programs, and projects contribute to making the world a more just, peaceful, and equitable place, as well as preserving our planet for generations to come?

8. Greenleaf, 53.

9. Chris Lowney, *Pope Francis: Why He Leads the Way He Leads* (Chicago: Loyola Press, 2013), 69.

This question provides a yardstick by which a leader can measure the positive impact of the ministry.

5. A Christian leader exercises participative management.

A good leader is a good listener who solicits ideas and insights from other members of the team. When possible, the leader allows the team to have influence over the decision-making process. "Insecure leaders hold back from consultation; they fear that by asking advice they will appear uninformed or vacillating, or that subordinates may come up with better ideas than the boss."[10]

The effective leader is a collaborator who puts the mission of the team ahead of any one individual. In this context, leading well means investing time and energy in building and sustaining a well-qualified, well-functioning team. It is not up to the leader to be an expert in every facet of the mission but to recognize, recruit, and motivate others on the team who possess the necessary information and skills to design and implement a successful ministry or project.

6. A Christian leader is a visionary.

Greenleaf connects a "visionary" quality of leadership to the gift displayed by the prophets in the Hebrew Scriptures. The prophets were not "fortune-tellers" in some magical sense. They were intelligent, insightful individuals with remarkable intuition. They were able to accurately assess the results that would derive from specific courses of action. Greenleaf believed that individuals with that same gift of prophecy are with us in every era of history, including the present.

> I now embrace the theory of prophecy, which holds that prophetic voices of great clarity, and with a quality of insight equal to that of any age, are speaking co-

10. Lowney, *Pope Francis*, 118.

gently all of the time. Men and women of a stature equal to the greatest of the past are with us now addressing the problems of the day and pointing to a better way. . . . The variable that marks some periods as barren and some as rich in prophetic vision is the interest, the level of seeking, the responsiveness of the hearers.[11]

Individuals with this gift for prophecy have a heightened sense of awareness, allowing them to "open wide the doors of perception so as to enable one to get more of what is available of sensory experience and other signals from the environment than people usually take in."[12]

Visionary leaders are responsible for helping set the vision that will guide the mission of the ministry and assist in designing individual projects with their teams. Be ready to recognize and affirm the visioning power of other team members when you see it.

7. A Christian leader leads by example.
A compelling vision and convincing words are important, but most importantly, an effective leader and leadership team lead by example. Walt Whitman wrote: "We convince by our presence." When our presence as leaders engenders confidence in those whom we lead—a confidence based upon values such as integrity, vision, determination, and confidence—those whom we are leading will trust us and want to work alongside us.

8. A Christian leader is a person of joy.
Our joy is from the Lord! "For I am convinced that neither death, nor life, nor angels, nor rulers, nor things present, nor things to come, nor powers, nor height, nor depth, nor

11. Greenleaf, *Servant Leadership*, 22.
12. Greenleaf, 40.

anything else in all creation, will be able to separate us from the love of God in Christ Jesus our Lord" (Rom 8:38-39 NRSV). This should create in us a feeling of irreplaceable joy. This quality of joy comes from living a life in harmony with the Spirit of God. This same quality is what keeps team members and volunteer leaders engaged.

I hope you are able to feel the pleasure that God receives from your ministry. And I hope you feel tremendous joy—the joy that comes from knowing that you are using gifts that have been uniquely given to you in order to give honor and glory to God. Always remember that you are working to ensure that the gospel message will be cherished and lived for generations to come in those whom you educate. Moreover, when challenging circumstances arise in your ministry or in your personal life, remember the one who has given you your joy—to cherish and to share.

9. A Christian leader is a good communicator.
Robert Greenleaf advocates for the importance of listening well: "only a true natural servant automatically responds to any problem by listening first. . . . I have seen enough remarkable transformation in people who have been trained to listen to have some confidence in this approach. It is because true listening builds strength in other people."[13] He reminds the reader of the words of St. Francis, "Lord, grant that I may not seek so much to be understood as to understand." Stephen Covey believed so strongly in the importance of listening well that he made it the fifth of his seven habits of highly effective people: Seek first to understand, then to be understood!

Effective communication involves answering the following questions: Who? What? When? Where? and How? The leader must determine who needs to be a part of the conver-

13. Greenleaf, 31.

sation, what the leader should say, when the conversation should happen, where the conversation should take place, and how it should happen or what tools should be used.

10. A Christian leader rests, relaxes, and rejuvenates.

One of the hardest disciplines to master is the self-discipline of taking time for "the three R's" of self-care—*rest*, *relax*, and *rejuvenate*. This self-care is necessary for all parts of one's life: the physical, mental, emotional, and spiritual aspects. A leader makes every effort to eat well, get plenty of sleep, take breaks that allow the mind to unwind and concentrate on things other than work, and participate in activities that feed the soul. In addition to taking breaks that allow one to pace oneself during a project or a particularly hectic time of ministry, it is important to plan for vacations and times of retreat. These are the opportunities that provide an extended period for applying "the three R's" of self-care.

Some leaders find it helpful to rely on someone who can assist them in applying these sound principles, such as a counselor or a spiritual director. Those whom you lead will notice the care you take of yourself. In that way, you will become a mentor for them. They will benefit from the example of a more balanced, more alert, and more pastoral leader.

11. A Christian leader is a person of prayer.

Prayer is our way of communicating with the divine, our way of building and strengthening the loving relationship that we have with the Lord. Love grows as relationships becoming stronger—with God, with others, and even with ourselves. Relationships are at the root of life and at the heart of love. The ideal way to build strong relationships is through prayer. God is always inviting us to enter more deeply into the relationship that each one of us shares with God—a relationship based on love, faith, and hope. Pastoral leaders transform lives—their own and others'—by helping people grow in their relationship with and love for God.

St. Ignatius of Loyola, the founder of the Jesuits, wrote: "All the things in this world are gifts of God, created for us to be the means by which we can come to know him better, love him more surely, and serve him more faithfully." Ignatius's spiritual principle of finding the divine in all of God's creation was further developed by Rev. James Bacik into a concept he calls "situational spirituality."

Situational spirituality has three underlying principles. First, we are oriented toward mystery. We are wired for God and restlessly search for the meaning of life. St. Augustine framed it in these words: "Our souls are restless, Lord, until they rest in you." We long for an intimate relationship with God. Second, we are interdependent social creatures, called to love others and to accept the love of others, especially God. Third, our outlook regarding creation is basically good. One could say, the grace of God interpenetrates us because we are each "temples of the Holy Spirit."

To develop a situational spirituality, one begins by asking questions such as: What am I dealing with? Where is God in this moment or this process? What would God want me to observe and to learn from this situation? By asking such questions, we are letting our lives write the agenda for our spiritual journeys. At that point, anything and everything that we experience has the potential to speak to us about God.

The principle of situational spirituality is an exciting and empowering way to live and to grow in our relationship with the Lord. A leader who can sense the presence of God in everything—sacred liturgy, beautiful music, fine art, the majesty of a sunset or a thunderstorm, the person standing close by—will more readily grasp the potential for God's handiwork in the design of a new project or relationship or leadership situation. Feeling the loving presence of God in such an intimate way, whether we are celebrating a joyful moment or suffering in a difficult circumstance, can give us tremendous comfort and reassurance.

God can and does speak to us in myriad ways at countless times during the course of each day. We begin to realize and appreciate this process once we have trained ourselves, with the help of God's grace, to have "eyes to see and ears to hear." It is one of the most important spiritual principles we can embrace and model for others.

A wonderful tool for applying the principles of situational spirituality is another Ignatian practice, the Daily Examen. In the Daily Examen, we mentally review the events of the day to see where the goodness of God was particularly present or where we failed to appreciate and act upon God's wisdom and grace. It is a simple and beautiful way to call to mind that God is in the midst of our day, even though we might not have realized it at the time. Here is a quick and easy way to practice the Daily Examen.

1. In the evening, find a quiet place to meditate by looking back on the events of the day in the company of the Holy Spirit. If parts of the day are confusing or if you cannot remember some aspects, ask God to bring clarity and understanding.

2. Review the day with a grateful heart. Remember, prayer is best begun with an attitude of gratitude. As you walk through the day, note the times of joy and delight. Focus on the day's gifts. Consider the work you accomplished and the people with whom you interacted. What did you receive from them? What did you give to them? Think about the details of the day, such as what you ate, what you saw, and so forth—remembering that God is in the details.

3. Pay attention to your emotions. One of the many great insights of Ignatius was his realization that we can often

detect the presence of the Holy Spirit in the movements of our emotions. Take time to reflect on the various emotions you experienced during the day. How might God have been speaking to you through those emotions?

4. Choose a specific feature of the day and pray it. Ask the Holy Spirit to guide you to a particular thought, feeling, or encounter from the day. It may be something striking or something that seemed insignificant at the time. Follow where the Spirit leads and take some time to pray about it. Allow the prayer to arise spontaneously from your heart—whether it is a prayer of intercession, praise, repentance, gratitude, surrender, or petition.

5. Look toward tomorrow. Ask God to give you wisdom and strength for the challenges the next day may present. Pay attention to the feelings that surface as you think about it. Are you excited, delighted, doubtful, anxious, or reluctant? Allow yourself to form these feelings into prayer(s). Seek God's guidance and pray for hope, courage, or whatever you feel is needed for the situations you may face. Ignatius encouraged people to talk to God as a friend. Sometime during the process, take a few moments to ask the Lord for forgiveness for your sins. Don't forget to do all of this in a spirit of gratitude. If time allows, end your Examen with the Lord's Prayer.[14]

All of the great leaders I have referenced in this chapter, both the secular and the religious, have recognized one very important concept. The great theologian and philosopher Teilhard de Chardin summarized it this way: "We are not human beings having a spiritual experience. We are spiri-

14. Adapted from "How Can I Pray?" (Chicago: Loyola Press, 2017), https://www.ignatianspirituality.com/ignatian-prayer/the-examen/how-can-i-pray/.

tual beings having a human experience." And prayer is a vitally important practice for every spiritual being. There are myriad ways to pray. Each leader must find the ways that best resonate with his or her life experience in building and sustaining a loving relationship with God, who loves us unconditionally. Here I have focused on one process, and an attendant practice of it, that has been particularly helpful for me as a Christian leader. No doubt you have discovered, and will continue to discover, the practices that work for you.

In Conclusion

Embracing a servant leadership approach helps us to imagine what is to come: " 'How do we get the right things done?' will be the watchword of the day, every day. And the context of those who bring it off will be this: all men and women who are touched by the effort grow taller, and become healthier, stronger, more autonomous *and* more disposed to serve."[15]

Charles Keating summarizes the spirituality of leadership in this way: "The effective leader is in a constant process of development, learning from his or her experience. . . . He or she accepts human nature as essentially relational, made as we are in the image and likeness of a relational God. He or she knows how to get jobs done while helping people feel their worth. . . . He or she appreciates the richness of diversity and helps others do the same . . . keeping a burning desire to better everything 'through Christ, with Christ and in Christ'. And like Christ, he or she will use all that is truly human to manifest the divine."[16]

15. Greenleaf, *Servant Leadership*, 60.
16. Charles Keating, *The Leadership Book* (Mahwah, NJ: Paulist Press, 1977), 132–33.

The Christian leader will find great joy and satisfaction in working with others, so that they may continue to progress in becoming the very best people that they can become for themselves, for others, and for God. This is what happens when we follow our passion, that fire in our souls that has been given to us by God. To be a Christian leader in a pastoral setting is "to care passionately that each successive generation will know Jesus Christ, the Good News he embodied, and the mission he commissioned to us."[17]

The Word was made flesh, dwelt among us, and now lovingly leads us forward as servant-leaders. We are bearers of the Word and builders of God's reign, right here, right now.

17. Tom Quinlan, *Excellence in Ministry: Best Practices for Successful Catechetical Leadership* (Chicago: Loyola Press, 2017), 141.

Reflection on the Pastoral Leadership Competencies

- Which of these competencies do you consider your greatest strengths as a pastoral leader?

- Which of these competencies do you want to improve or enhance as a pastoral leader?

- How can you develop a personal learning plan to strengthen the areas you identified for growth as a pastoral leader?

A Select Resource Guide to Digital Ministry

Anderson, Keith. *The Digital Cathedral: Networked Ministry in a Wireless World*. New York: Morehouse, 2015.

Anderson, Keith, and Elizabeth Drescher. *Click2Save Reboot: The Digital Ministry Bible*. New York: Church Publishing, 2018.

Caldwell, Cath. *Graphic Design for Everyone: Understand the Building Blocks so You Can Do It Yourself*. New York: DK Illustrated Edition, 2019.

Campbell, Heidi. *The Distanced Church: Reflections on Doing Church Online*. Digital Religion Publications. 2020. https://hdl.handle.net/1969.1/187970.

Campbell, Heidi. *Religion in Quarantine: The Future of Religion in a Post-Pandemic World.* Digital Religion Publications. 2020. https://hdl.handle.net/1969.1/188004.

Campbell, Heidi, ed. *Revisiting the Distanced Church*. Digital Religion Publications. 2020. https://hdl.handle.net/1969.1/193368.

Campbell, Heidi, and Troy Shepherd, eds. *What Should Post-Pandemic Religion Look Like?* Digital Religion Publications. 2020. https://hdl.handle.net/1969.1/192408.

Crouch, Amy, and Andy Crouch. *My Tech-Wise Life: Growing Up and Making Choices in a World of Devices*. Grand Rapids, MI: Baker, 2020.

Crouch, Andy. *The Tech-Wise Family: Everyday Steps for Putting Technology in Its Proper Place*. Grand Rapids, MI: Baker, 2017.

Gorrell, Angela. *Always On: Practicing Faith in a New Media Landscape*. Grand Rapids, MI: Baker Academic, 2019.

Jones, Nona. *From Social Media to Social Ministry: A Guide to Digital Discipleship*. Grand Rapids, MI: Zondervan, 2020.

Krug, Steve. *Don't Make Me Think: A Common Sense Approach to Web Usability*. 3rd ed. Berkeley: New Riders, 2014.

"Leading Ideas." Lewis Center for Church Leadership. www.churchleadership.com/tag/online-ministry.

Lombardozzi, Catherine. *Learning Environments by Design*. Alexandria, VA: ATD Press, 2015.

Panzer, Ryan M. *Grace and Gigabytes: Being Church in a Tech-Shaped Culture*. Minneapolis: Fortress Press, 2020.

Thompson, Deanna A. *The Virtual Body of Christ in a Suffering World*. Nashville: Abingdon, 2016.

Williams, Robin. *The Non-Designer's Design Book*. 4th ed. San Francisco: Peachpit Press, 2014.